Thornton Wilder
Our Town

A Play in Three Acts

Herausgegeben von
Eva-Maria König

Philipp Reclam jun. Stuttgart

Universal-Bibliothek Nr. 9168
Alle Rechte vorbehalten
© für diese Ausgabe 1984 Philipp Reclam jun. GmbH & Co.,
Stuttgart
© für den Text 1938, 1957 by Thornton Wilder
Our Town is the sole property of the author and is fully
protected by copyright. It may not be acted by professionals or
amateurs without formal permission and the payment of a
royalty. All rights, including professional, amateur, stock, ra-
dio and television, broadcasting, motion picture, recitation,
lecturing, public reading, and the rights of translation into
foreign languages are reserved. All English language inquiries
should be addressed to Harold Freedman, Brandt & Brandt
Dramatic Department, Inc. 1501 Broadway, New York, N. Y.
10036. All German language inquiries should be addressed to
S. Fischer Verlag, Frankfurt a. M.
Gesamtherstellung: Reclam, Ditzingen. Printed in Germany 1998
RECLAM und UNIVERSAL-BIBLIOTHEK sind eingetragene
Marken der Philipp Reclam jun. GmbH & Co., Stuttgart
ISBN 3-15-009168-3

Our Town

Characters
(in the order of their appearance)

STAGE MANAGER
DR. GIBBS
5 JOE CROWELL
HOWIE NEWSOME
MRS. GIBBS
MRS. WEBB
GEORGE GIBBS
10 REBECCA GIBBS
WALLY WEBB
EMILY WEBB
PROFESSOR WILLARD
MR. WEBB
15 WOMAN IN THE BALCONY
MAN IN THE AUDITORIUM
LADY IN THE BOX
SIMON STIMSON
MRS. SOAMES
20 CONSTABLE WARREN
SI CROWELL
THREE BASEBALL PLAYERS
SAM CRAIG
JOE STODDARD

25 *The entire play takes place in Grover's Corners, New Hampshire.*

3 **stage manager:** Spielleiter, Regisseur.
15 **balcony:** hier: Rang.
16 **auditorium:** Zuschauerraum.
17 **box:** hier: Loge.
20 **constable:** Polizist, Schutzmann.

Act I

No curtain.
No scenery.
The audience, arriving, sees an empty stage in half-light.
5 *Presently the stage manager, hat on and pipe in mouth,*
enters and begins placing a table and three chairs down-
stage left, and a table and three chairs downstage right.
He also places a low bench at the corner of what will be
the Webb house, left.
10 *"Left" and "right" are from the point of view of the actor*
facing the audience. "Up" is toward the back wall.
As the house lights go down he has finished setting the
stage and leaning against the right proscenium pillar
watches the late arrivals in the audience.
15 *When the auditorium is in complete darkness he speaks:*

STAGE MANAGER. This play is called "Our Town". It was
written by Thornton Wilder; produced and directed
by A. ... (or produced by A. ...; directed by
B. ...). In it you will see Miss C. ...; Miss D. ...;
20 Miss E. ...; and Mr. F. ...; Mr. G. ...; Mr. H. ...;
and many others. The name of the town is Grover's Corners, New Hampshire – just across the

---

3 **scenery:** Bühnendekoration, Szenerie.
6 f. **downstage:** vorn auf der Bühne (Gegensatz: *upstage*).
13 **proscenium:** Vorderbühne, Vorderbühnen-.
pillar: Pfeiler, Säule.
17 **to produce:** inszenieren, zur Aufführung bringen.
to direct: Regie führen, leiten.

Massachusetts line: latitude 42 degrees 40 minutes;
longitude 70 degrees 37 minutes. The First Act shows
a day in our town. The day is May 7, 1901. The time is
just before dawn.

5   *(A rooster crows.)*
The sky is beginning to show some streaks of light
over in the East there, behind our mount'in.
The morning star always gets wonderful bright the
minute before it has to go – doesn't it?

10 *(He stares at it for a moment, then goes upstage.)*
Well, I'd better show you how our town lies. Up
here – *(that is: parallel with the back wall)* is Main
Street. Way back there is the railway station; tracks
go that way. Polish Town's across the tracks, and

15 some Canuck families.
(Toward the left.)
Over there is the Congregational Church; across the
street's the Presbyterian.
Methodist and Unitarian are over there.

20 Baptist is down in the holla' by the river.

---

1 **latitude:** (geographische) Breite.
2 **longitude:** (geographische) Länge.
5 **rooster** (AE): Hahn.
6 **streak:** Streifen.
13 **way back:** weit hinten.
14 **Polish Town:** das polnische Viertel.
15 **Canuck:** Slangwort für (französischstämmige) Kanadier.
17 **Congregational:** kongregationalistisch (kalvinistisch orientierte Ein-
   zelgemeinden ohne übergeordnete Kirchenstruktur).
18 **Presbyterian:** presbyterianisch.
19 **Methodist:** methodistisch.
   Unitarian: unitarisch.
20 **Baptist:** baptistisch.
   holla' (= *hollow*): Senke, Tal.

Catholic Church is over beyond the tracks.

Here's the Town Hall and Post Office combined; jail's in the basement.

Bryan once made a speech from these very steps
5 here.

Along here's a row of stores. Hitching posts and horse blocks in front of them. First automobile's going to come along in about five years – belonged to Banker Cartwright, our richest citizen . . . lives in the
10 big white house up on the hill.

Here's the grocery store and here's Mr. Morgan's drugstore. Most everybody in town manages to look into those two stores once a day.

Public School's over yonder. High School's still
15 farther over. Quarter of nine mornings, noontimes, and three o'clock afternoons, the hull town can hear the yelling and screaming from those school-yards.

(He approaches the table and chairs downstage right.)
20 This is our doctor's house, – Doc Gibbs'. This is the back door.

2 **Town Hall:** Rathaus.
3 **jail:** Gefängnis.
  basement: Keller(geschoß).
4 **Bryan:** William Jennings B. (1860–1925), amerikanischer Politiker.
6 **store:** Laden (AE).
  hitching post: Anbindepfosten (für Pferde).
7 **horse block:** Aufsitzblock.
9 **banker:** Bankier.
11 **grocery store:** Kolonialwarenhandlung.
14 **Public School:** staatliche Schule, Grundschule (AE).
  over yonder: dort drüben.
  High School: höhere Schule (AE).
15 **quarter of nine** (AE): *quarter to nine.*
16 **hull:** *whole.*

*(Two arched trellises, covered with vines and flowers,
are pushed out, one by each proscenium pillar.)*
There's some scenery for those who think they have
to have scenery.
5   This is Mrs. Gibbs' garden. Corn ... peas ...
beans ... hollyhocks ... heliotrope ... and a lot of
burdock.
(Crosses the stage.)
In those days our newspaper come out twice a week –
10   the Grover's Corners *Sentinel* – and this is Editor
Webb's house.
And this is Mrs. Webb's garden.
Just like Mrs. Gibbs', only it's got a lot of sunflowers,
too.
15   *(He looks upward, center stage.)*
Right here ... 's a big butternut tree.
*(He returns to his place by the right proscenium pillar
and looks at the audience for a minute.)*
Nice Town, y'know what I mean?
20   Nobody very remarkable ever come out of it, s'far as
we know.
The earliest tombstones in the cemetery up there on
the mountain say 1670–1680 – they're Grovers and

---

1 **arched:** von *arch* ›Bogen‹.
  trellis: Spalier.
5 **corn:** Mais (AE).
6 **hollyhock:** Stockrose, Rosenmalve.
  heliotrope: Heliotrop, Sonnenwende (Pflanze).
7 **burdock:** Klette.
10 **sentinel:** (Schild-)Wache.
  editor: Herausgeber, Redakteur.
16 **butternut:** Butternuß (nordamerikanische Walnußart).
22 **tombstone:** Grabstein.
  cemetery: Friedhof.

Cartwrights and Gibbses and Herseys – same names
as are around here now.

Well, as I said: it's about dawn.

The only lights on in town are in a cottage over by the
tracks where a Polish mother's just had twins. And in
the Joe Crowell house, where Joe Junior's getting up
so as to deliver the paper. And in the depot, where
Shorty Hawkins is gettin' ready to flag the 5:45 for
Boston.

*(A train whistle is heard. The stage manager takes out
his watch and nods.)*

Naturally, out in the country – all around – there've
been lights on for some time, what with milkin's and
so on. But town people sleep late.

So – another day's begun.

There's Doc Gibbs comin' down Main Street now,
comin' back from that baby case. And here's his wife
comin' downstairs to get breakfast.

*(Mrs. Gibbs, a plump, pleasant woman in the middle
thirties, comes "downstairs" right. She pulls up an
imaginary window shade in her kitchen and starts to
make a fire in her stove.)*

Doc Gibbs died in 1930. The new hospital's named
after him.

Mrs. Gibbs died first – long time ago, in fact. She
went out to visit her daughter, Rebecca, who married

---

5 **twin:** Zwilling.
7 **depot:** Bahnhof (AE).
8 **to flag:** hier: abfahren lassen (durch ein Signal mit einer Fahne).
13 **what with:** wegen.
19 **plump:** rundlich, mollig, drall.
21 **imaginary:** imaginär, nicht wirklich vorhanden.
   window shade: Vorhang, Rollo.

an insurance man in Canton, Ohio, and died there –
pneumonia – but her body was brought back here.
She's up in the cemetery there now – in with a whole
mess of Gibbses and Herseys – she was Julia Hersey
'fore she married Doc Gibbs in the Congregational
Church over there.
In our town we like to know the facts about everybody.
There's Mrs. Webb, coming downstairs to get her
breakfast, too.
That's Doc Gibbs. Got that call at half past one this
morning.
And there comes Joe Crowell, Jr., delivering Mr.
Webb's *Sentinel*.
*(Dr. Gibbs has been coming along Main Street from
the left. At the point where he would turn to approach
his house, he stops, sets down his – imaginary – black
bag, takes off his hat, and rubs his face with fatigue,
using an enormous handkerchief.*
*Mrs. Webb, a thin, serious, crisp woman, has entered
her kitchen, left, tying on an apron. She goes through
the motions of putting wood into a stove, lighting it,
and preparing breakfast.*
*Suddenly, Joe Crowell, Jr., eleven, starts down Main
Street from the right, hurling imaginary newspapers
into doorways.)*
JOE CROWELL, JR. Morning, Doc Gibbs.

---

1 **insurance:** Versicherung.
2 **pneumonia:** Lungenentzündung.
4 **mess:** Durcheinander.
18 **fatigue:** Ermüdung.
20 **crisp:** frisch; entschieden, sachlich.
25 **to hurl:** schleudern, kräftig werfen.

DR. GIBBS. Morning, Joe.

JOE CROWELL, JR. Somebody been sick, Doc?

DR. GIBBS. No. Just some twins born over in Polish Town.

JOE CROWELL, JR. Do you want your paper now?

5 DR. GIBBS. Yes, I'll take it. – Anything serious goin' on in the world since Wednesday?

JOE CROWELL, JR. Yessir. My schoolteacher, Miss Foster, 's getting married to a fella over in Concord.

DR. GIBBS. I declare. – How do you boys feel about that?

10 JOE CROWELL, JR. Well, of course, it's none of my business – but I think if a person starts out to be a teacher, she ought to stay one.

DR. GIBBS. How's your knee, Joe?

JOE CROWELL, JR. Fine, Doc, I never think about it at all.
15 Only like you said, it always tells me when it's going to rain.

DR. GIBBS. What's it telling you today? Goin' to rain?

JOE CROWELL, JR. No, sir.

DR. GIBBS. Sure?

20 JOE CROWELL, JR. Yessir.

DR. GIBBS. Knee ever make a mistake?

JOE CROWELL, JR. No, sir.

(Joe goes off. Dr. Gibbs stands reading his paper.)

STAGE MANAGER. Want to tell you something about that
25 boy Joe Crowell there. Joe was awful bright – graduated from high school here, head of his class. So he

---

8 **fella:** *fellow.*

9 **I declare:** Na sieh mal an; Ich muß schon sagen; Wahrhaftig.

11 **to start out to do s.th.:** sich etwas vornehmen, etwas anfangen.

25 **awful bright** (coll.): *awfully bright.* Zur Verwendung des Adjektivs als Adverb vgl. auch 15,11 *special,* 17,2 *gradual* und 30,27 f. *serious/ seriously.*

25 f. **to graduate:** einen Schul-(Universitäts-)Abschluß machen.

got a scholarship to Massachusetts Tech. Graduated
head of his class there, too. It was all wrote up in the
Boston paper at the time. Goin' to be a great
engineer, Joe was. But the war broke out and he died
5   in France. – All that education for nothing.

HOWIE NEWSOME *(off left)*. Giddap, Bessie! What's the
matter with you today?

STAGE MANAGER. Here comes Howie Newsome, de-
liverin' the milk.

10 *(Howie Newsome, about thirty, in overalls, comes
along Main Street from the left, walking beside an
invisible horse and wagon and carrying an imaginary
rack with milk bottles. The sound of clinking milk
bottles is heard. He leaves some bottles at Mrs. Webb's
15 trellis, then, crossing the stage to Mrs. Gibbs', he stops
center to talk to Dr. Gibbs.)*

HOWIE NEWSOME. Morning, Doc.

DR. GIBBS. Morning, Howie.

HOWIE NEWSOME. Somebody sick?

20 DR. GIBBS. Pair of twins over to Mrs. Goruslawski's.

HOWIE NEWSOME. Twins, eh? This town's gettin' bigger
every year.

DR. GIBBS. Goin' to rain, Howie?

HOWIE NEWSOME. No, no. Fine day – that'll burn
25 through. Come on, Bessie.

DR. GIBBS. Hello Bessie.

---

1 **scholarship:** Stipendium
  Tech.: Kurzform für *Technical College*.
6 **giddap:** *get up*.
13 **rack:** Ständer.
  to clink: klirren.
24 f. **to burn through:** hier: sonnig werden.

(He strokes the horse, which has remained up center.)
How old is she, Howie?

HOWIE NEWSOME. Going on seventeen. Bessie's all mixed
up about the route ever since the Lockharts stopped
5 takin' their quart of milk every day. She wants to
leave 'em a quart just the same – keeps scolding me
the hull trip.
*(He reaches Mrs. Gibbs' back door. She is waiting for
him.)*

10 MRS. GIBBS. Good morning, Howie.

HOWIE NEWSOME. Morning, Mrs. Gibbs. Doc's just
comin' down the street.

MRS. GIBBS. Is he? Seems like you're late today.

HOWIE NEWSOME. Yes. Somep'n went wrong with the
15 separator. Don't know what 'twas.
(He passes Dr. Gibbs up center.)
Doc!

DR. GIBBS. Howie!

MRS. GIBBS *(calling upstairs).* Children! Children! Time
20 to get up.

HOWIE NEWSOME. Come on, Bessie!
(He goes off right.)

MRS. GIBBS. George! Rebecca!
*(Dr. Gibbs arrives at his back door and passes
25 through the trellis into his house.)*

MRS. GIBBS. Everything all right, Frank?

DR. GIBBS. Yes. I declare – easy as kittens.

---

1 **to stroke:** streicheln.
5 **quart:** Quart (amerikanisches Hohlmaß, 0,946 l).
6 **to scold:** schelten.
14 **somep'n:** *something.*
15 **separator:** (Milch-)Zentrifuge.
27 **kitten:** Kätzchen, Katzenjunges.

MRS. GIBBS. Bacon'll be ready in a minute. Set down and drink your coffee. You can catch a couple hours' sleep this morning, can't you?

DR. GIBBS. Hm! . . . Mrs. Wentworth's coming at eleven.
5   Guess I know what it's about, too. Her stummick ain't what it ought to be.

MRS. GIBBS. All told, you won't get more'n three hours' sleep. Frank Gibbs, I don't know what's goin' to become of you. I do wish I could get you to go away some-
10   place and take a rest. I think it would do you good.

MRS. WEBB. Emileeee! Time to get up! Wally! Seven o'clock!

MRS. GIBBS. I declare, you got to speak to George. Seems like something's come over him lately. He's no help
15   to me at all. I can't even get him to cut me some wood.

DR. GIBBS. *(Washing and drying his hands at the sink. Mrs. Gibbs is busy at the stove.)* Is he sassy to you?

MRS. GIBBS. No. He just whines! All he thinks about is
20   that baseball – George! Rebecca! You'll be late for school.

DR. GIBBS. M-m-m . . .

MRS. GIBBS. George!

DR. GIBBS. George, look sharp!

---

1 **set down:** *sit down.*
5 (*I*) **guess:** ich nehme an, ich glaube (AE).
   stummick: *stomach.*
7 **all told:** alles in allem.
   more'n: *more than.*
17 **sink:** Spüle, Spültisch.
18 **sassy:** frech, unverschämt.
19 **to whine:** wimmern, jammern.
24 **look sharp!:** mach schnell!

GEORGE'S VOICE. Yes, Pa!

DR. GIBBS *(as he goes off the stage)*. Don't you hear your
  mother calling you? I guess I'll go upstairs and get
  forty winks.

5 MRS. WEBB. Walleee! Emileee! You'll be late for school!
  Walleee! You wash yourself good or I'll come up and
  do it myself.

REBECCA GIBBS' VOICE. Ma! What dress shall I wear?

MRS. GIBBS. Don't make a noise. Your father's been out
10 all night and needs his sleep. I washed and ironed the
  blue gingham for you special.

REBECCA. Ma, I hate that dress.

MRS. GIBBS. Oh, hush-up-with-you.

REBECCA. Every day I go to school dressed like a sick
15 turkey.

MRS. GIBBS. Now, Rebecca, you always look *very* nice.

REBECCA. Mama, George's throwing soap at me.

MRS. GIBBS. I'll come and slap the both of you, – that's
  what I'll do.

20 *(A factory whistle sounds.*
  The children dash in and take their places at the tables.
  Right, George, about sixteen, and Rebecca, eleven.
  Left, Emily and Wally, same ages. They carry strap-
  ped schoolbooks.)

25 STAGE MANAGER. We've got a factory in our town too –

---

3 f. **to get forty winks:** ein Nickerchen machen.
11 **gingham:** Gingan (gestreifter Baumwollstoff), Gingan-Kleid.
15 **turkey:** Truthahn.
16 **now:** hier: na hör mal.
18 **to slap:** schlagen, ohrfeigen.
21 **to dash:** stürzen, rennen, jagen.
23 f. **strapped:** zusammengeschnürt, mit einem Riemen zusammengebunden.

hear it? Makes blankets. Cartwrights own it and it brung 'em a fortune.

MRS. WEBB. Children! Now I won't have it. Breakfast is just as good as any other meal and I won't have you
5 gobbling like wolves. It'll stunt your growth, – that's a fact. Put away your book, Wally.

WALLY. Aw, Ma! By ten o'clock I got to know all about Canada.

MRS. WEBB. You know the rule's well as I do – no books
10 at table. As for me, I'd rather have my children healthy than bright.

EMILY. I'm both, Mama: you know I am. I'm the brightest girl in school for my age. I have a wonderful memory.

15 MRS. WEBB. Eat your breakfast.

WALLY. I'm bright, too, when I'm looking at my stamp collection.

MRS. GIBBS. I'll speak to your father about it when he's rested. Seems to me twenty-five cents a week's
20 enough for a boy your age. I declare I don't know how you spend it all.

GEORGE. Aw, Ma, – I gotta lotta things to buy.

MRS. GIBBS. Strawberry phosphates – that's what you spend it on.

25 GEORGE. I don't see how Rebecca comes to have so much money. She has more'n a dollar.

---

2 **brung** (coll.): *brought*.
5 **to gobble:** schlingen, gierig essen.
  to stunt: behindern, verkümmern lassen.
22 **I gotta lotta things to buy:** *I have got a lot of things to buy*.
23 **strawberry phosphate:** Erdbeerlimonade, Erdbeergetränk mit Phosphatzusatz.

REBECCA *(spoon in mouth, dreamily)*. I've been saving it up gradual.

MRS. GIBBS. Well, dear, I think it's a good thing to spend some every now and then.

5 REBECCA. Mama, do you know what I love most in the world – do you? – Money.

MRS. GIBBS. Eat your breakfast.

THE CHILDREN. Mama, there's first bell. – I gotta hurry. – I don't want any more. – I gotta hurry.

10 *(The children rise, seize their books and dash out through the trellises. They meet, down center, and chattering, walk to Main Street, then turn left.*
The stage manager goes off, unobtrusively, right.)

MRS. WEBB. Walk fast, but you don't have to run. Wally,
15 pull up your pants at the knee. Stand up straight, Emily.

MRS. GIBBS. Tell Miss Foster I send her my best congratulations – can you remember that?

REBECCA. Yes, Ma.

20 MRS. GIBBS. You look real nice, Rebecca. Pick up your feet.

ALL. Good-by.

(Mrs. Gibbs fills her apron with food for the chickens and comes down to the footlights.)

25 MRS. GIBBS. Here, chick, chick, chick.

---

12 **to chatter:** schwatzen.
13 **unobtrusively** (adv.): unaufdringlich, unauffällig.
15 **pants** (pl.): Hose (AE).
   Stand up straight: Halt dich gerade.
17f. **congratulations:** Glückwünsche.
22 **good-by:** im AE geläufige Variante zu *good-bye.*
24 **footlights:** Rampe(nlicht).

No, go away, you. Go away.

Here, chick, chick, chick.

What's the matter with *you*? Fight, fight, fight, –
that's all you do. Hm ... *you* don't belong to me.

5　Where'd you come from?

(She shakes her apron.)

Oh, don't be so scared. Nobody's going to hurt you.

*(Mrs. Webb is sitting on the bench by her trellis,
stringing beans.)*

10　Good morning, Myrtle. How's your cold?

MRS. WEBB. Well, I still get that tickling feeling in my
throat. I told Charles I didn't know as I'd go to choir
practice tonight. Wouldn't be any use.

MRS. GIBBS. Have you tried singing over your voice?

15　MRS. WEBB. Yes, but somehow I can't do that and stay on
the key. While I'm resting myself I thought I'd string
some of these beans.

MRS. GIBBS *(rolling up her sleeves as she crosses the stage
for a chat)*. Let me help you. Beans have been good

20　this year.

MRS. WEBB. I've decided to put up forty quarts if it kills
me. The children say they hate 'em, but I notice
they're able to get 'em down all winter.

(Pause. Brief sound of chickens cackling.)

9　**to string:** abziehen, putzen.
11　**to tickle:** kitzeln.
12 f. **choir practice:** Chorprobe.
14 **to sing over one's voice:** mit besonders lauter Stimme singen.
15 f. **to stay on the key:** den Ton halten.
19　**chat:** Schwätzchen.
21 **to put up:** einmachen.
21 f. **if it kills me:** auf jeden Fall.
24 **to cackle:** gackern.

MRS. GIBBS. Now, Myrtle. I've got to tell you something, because if I don't tell somebody I'll burst.

MRS. WEBB. Why, Julia Gibbs!

MRS. GIBBS. Here, give me some more of those beans.
5 Myrtle, did one of those secondhand-furniture men from Boston come to see you last Friday?

MRS. WEBB. No-o.

MRS. GIBBS. Well, he called on me. First I thought he was a patient wantin' to see Dr. Gibbs. 'N he wormed his
10 way into my parlor, and, Myrtle Webb, he offered me three hundred and fifty dollars for Grandmother Wentworth's highboy, as I'm sitting here!

MRS. WEBB. Why, Julia Gibbs!

MRS. GIBBS. He did! That old thing! Why, it was so big I
15 didn't know where to put it and I almost give it to Cousin Hester Wilcox.

MRS. WEBB. Well, you're going to take it, aren't you?

MRS. GIBBS. I don't know.

MRS. WEBB. You don't know – three hundred and fifty
20 dollars! What's come over you?

MRS. GIBBS. Well, if I could get the Doctor to take the money and go away someplace on a real trip, I'd sell it like that. – Y'know, Myrtle, it's been the dream of my life to see Paris, France. – Oh, I don't know. It
25 sounds crazy, I suppose, but for years I've been promising myself that if we ever had the chance –

MRS. WEBB. How does the Doctor feel about it?

MRS. GIBBS. Well, I did beat about the bush a little and

---

9 **'n:** *and.*

9f. **to worm one's way into:** sich einschleichen.

12 **highboy** (AE): Aufsatzkommode.

23 **like that:** hier: sofort, im Nu.

said that if I got a legacy – that's the way I put it – I'd
make him take me somewhere.

MRS. WEBB. M-m-m . . . What did he say?

MRS. GIBBS. You know how he is. I haven't heard a
5   serious word out of him since I've known him. No, he
said, it might make him discontented with Grover's
Corners to go traipsin' about Europe; better let well
enough alone, he says. Every two years he makes a
trip to the battlefields of the Civil War and that's
10   enough treat for anybody, he says.

MRS. WEBB. Well, Mr. Webb just *admires* the way Dr.
Gibbs knows everything about the Civil War. Mr.
Webb's a good mind to give up Napoleon and move
over to the Civil War, only Dr. Gibbs being one of
15   the greatest experts in the country just makes him
despair.

MRS. GIBBS. It's a fact! Dr. Gibbs is never so happy as
when he's at Antietam or Gettysburg. The times I've
walked over those hills, Myrtle, stopping at every
20   bush and pacing it all out, like we were going to
buy it.

MRS. WEBB. Well, if that secondhand man's really serious
about buyin' it, Julia, you sell it. And then you'll get
to see Paris, all right. Just keep droppin' hints from
25   time to time – that's how I got to see the Atlantic
Ocean, y'know.

---

  1 **legacy:** Erbschaft.
  6 **discontented:** unzufrieden.
  7 **to traipse:** bummeln, schlendern.
  7 f. **let well enough alone:** zufrieden sein mit dem, was man hat.
 10 **treat:** Genuß, Fest.
 18 **Antietam / Gettysburg:** berühmte Schauplätze des Amerikanischen
    Bürgerkriegs.

MRS. GIBBS. Oh, I'm sorry I mentioned it. Only it seems
to me that once in your life before you die you ought
to see a country where they don't talk in English and
don't even want to.

5 *(The stage manager enters briskly from the right. He
tips his hat to the ladies, who nod their heads.)*

STAGE MANAGER. Thank you, ladies. Thank you very much.
*(Mrs. Gibbs and Mrs. Webb gather up their things,
return into their homes and disappear.)*

10 Now we're going to skip a few hours.
But first we want a little more information about the
town, kind of a scientific account, you might say.
So I've asked Professor Willard of our State University to sketch in a few details of our past history here.

15 Is Professor Willard here?
*(Professor Willard, a rural savant, pince-nez on a
wide satin ribbon, enters from the right with some
notes in his hand.)*

May I introduce Professor Willard of our State Uni-

20 versity.
A few brief notes, thank you, Professor, – unfortu-
nately our time is limited.

PROFESSOR WILLARD. Grover's Corners ... let me see ...
Grover's Corners lies on the old Pleistocene

---

5 **briskly** (adv.): lebhaft, munter.
6 **to tip:** antippen.
10 **to skip:** überspringen.
14 **to sketch:** umreißen, skizzieren.
16 **rural:** ländlich, vom Lande.
   savant: Gelehrter.
   pince-nez (frz.): Kneifer.
17 **satin:** Atlasseide, Satin.
24 **Pleistocene:** (Geol.) pleistozän, Pleistozän- (aus dem Eiszeitalter
   stammend).

granite of the Appalachian range. I may say it's some
of the oldest land in the world. We're very proud of
that. A shelf of Devonian basalt crosses it with ves-
tiges of Mesozoic shale, and some sandstone outcrop-
5   pings; but that's all more recent: two hundred, three
hundred million years old.

Some highly interesting fossils have been found . . . I
may say: unique fossils . . . two miles out of town, in
Silas Peckham's cow pasture. They can be seen at the
10   museum in our University at any time – that is, at any
reasonable time. Shall I read some of Professor
Gruber's notes on the meteorological situation –
mean precipitation, et cetera?

STAGE MANAGER. Afraid we won't have time for that,
15   Professor. We might have a few words on the history
of man here.

PROFESSOR WILLARD. Yes . . . anthropological data:
Early Amerindian stock. Cotahatchee tribes . . . no
evidence before the tenth century of this era . . .

---

1 **granite:** Granit.
3 **shelf:** Platte, Sockel.
   Devonian: (Geol.) devonisch, Devon- (aus dem erdgeschichtlichen
   Altertum stammend).
3f. **vestige:** Spur, Rest.
4 **Mesozoic:** (Geol.) mesozoisch (aus dem Erdmittelalter).
   shale: Schieferton.
4f. **outcropping:** Ausläufer, an die Oberfläche tretende Schicht.
7 **fossil:** Fossilie, Versteinerung.
8 **unique:** einzigartig.
13 **mean:** mittlere(r, -s), Durchschnitts-.
   precipitation: Niederschlag.
17 **data:** Daten, Angaben.
18 **Amerindian:** aus *American* und *Indian* ›Indianer, indianisch‹.
   stock: Stamm, Rasse.
19 **evidence:** Nachweis.

hm ... now entirely disappeared ... possible traces
in three families. Migration toward the end of the
seventeenth century of English brachiocephalic blue-
eyed stock ... for the most part. Since then some
5 Slav and Mediterranean –

STAGE MANAGER. And the population, Professor Willard?

PROFESSOR WILLARD. Within the town limits: 2,640.

STAGE MANAGER. Just a moment, Professor.

10 *(He whispers into the professor's ear.)*

PROFESSOR WILLARD. Oh, yes, indeed? – The population,
at the moment, is 2,642. The Postal District brings in 507
more, making a total of 3,149. – Mortality and birth
rates: constant. – By MacPherson's gauge: 6.032.

15 STAGE MANAGER. Thank you very much, Professor.
We're all very much obliged to you, I'm sure.

PROFESSOR WILLARD. Not at all, sir; not at all.

STAGE MANAGER. This way, Professor, and thank you
again.

20 *(Exit Professor Willard.)*
Now the political and social report: Editor Webb. –
Oh, Mr. Webb?
(Mrs. Webb appears at her back door.)

MRS. WEBB. He'll be here in a minute. . . . He just cut his
25 hand while he was eatin' an apple.

---

2 **migration:** (Ein-, Zu-)Wanderung.
3 **brachiocephalic:** brachyzephal, kurzschädelig.
5 **Slav:** slawisch.
   Mediterranean: Mittelmeer-.
13 **mortality:** Sterblichkeit.
14 **gauge:** Maßstab.
16 **obliged:** verbunden, (zu Dank) verpflichtet.
20 **exit:** geht ab.

STAGE MANAGER. Thank you, Mrs. Webb.

MRS. WEBB. Charles! Everybody's waitin'.

(Exit Mrs. Webb.)

STAGE MANAGER. Mr. Webb is Publisher and Editor of
5   the Grover's Corners *Sentinel*. That's our local paper,
y'know.

*(Mr. Webb enters from his house, pulling on his coat.
His finger is bound in a handkerchief.)*

MR. WEBB. Well . . . I don't have to tell you that we're
10   run here by a Board of Selectmen. – All males vote at
the age of twenty-one. Women vote indirect. We're
lower middle class: sprinkling of professional men . . .
ten per cent illiterate laborers. Politically, we're
eighty-six per cent Republicans; six per cent Demo-
15   crats; four per cent Socialists; rest, indifferent.
Religiously, we're eighty-five per cent Protestants;
twelve per cent Catholics; rest, indifferent.

STAGE MANAGER. Have you any comments, Mr. Webb?

MR. WEBB. Very ordinary town, if you ask me. Little
20   better behaved than most. Probably a lot duller.
But our young people here seem to like it well
enough. Ninety per cent of 'em graduating from high
school settle down right here to live – even when
they've been away to college.

25 STAGE MANAGER. Now, is there anyone in the audience

---

4 **publisher:** Verleger, Herausgeber.
10 **board:** Gremium, Ausschuß.
   selectman (AE): Stadtrat, Magistratsperson.
12 **sprinkling:** Spritzer; hier: ein paar, einzelne.
   professional man: Geistesarbeiter, in höheren Berufsständen Täti-
   ger, Akademiker.
13 **illiterate:** analphabetisch, ungebildet.
18 **comment:** Erläuterung, Anmerkung.

who would like to ask Editor Webb anything about
the town?

WOMAN IN THE BALCONY. Is there much drinking in Grover's Corners?

5 MR. WEBB. Well, ma'am, I wouldn't know what you'd
call *much*. Satiddy nights the farmhands meet down
in Ellery Greenough's stable and holler some. We've
got one or two town drunks, but they're always
having remorses every time an evangelist comes to
10 town. No, ma'am, I'd say likker ain't a regular thing
in the home here, except in the medicine chest. Right
good for snake bite, y'know – always was.

BELLIGERENT MAN AT BACK OF AUDITORIUM. Is there no
one in town aware of –

15 STAGE MANAGER. Come forward, will you, where we can
all hear you – What were you saying?

BELLIGERENT MAN. Is there no one in town aware of
social injustice and industrial inequality?

MR. WEBB. Oh, yes, everybody is – somethin' terrible.
20 Seems like they spend most of their time talking
about who's rich and who's poor.

BELLIGERENT MAN. Then why don't they do something
about it?

(He withdraws without waiting for an answer.)

---

6 **Satiddy:** *Saturday.*
   farmhand: Landarbeiter.
7 **to holler:** schreien, brüllen.
8 **drunk:** Betrunkener, Trunkenbold.
9 **remorse:** Gewissensbiß.
   evangelist: Wanderprediger.
10 **likker** (= *liquor*): Alkohol, alkoholische(s) Getränk(e).
13 **belligerent:** angriffslustig, streitbar.
18 **inequality:** Ungleichheit.

MR. WEBB. Well, I dunno. .... I guess we're all hunting like everybody else for a way the diligent and sensible can rise to the top and the lazy and quarrelsome can sink to the bottom. But it ain't easy to find. Mean-
5   while, we do all we can to help those that can't help themselves and those that can we leave alone. – Are there any other questions?

LADY IN A BOX. Oh, Mr. Webb? Mr. Webb, is there any culture or love of beauty in Grover's Corners?

10 MR. WEBB. Well, ma'am, there ain't much – not in the sense you mean. Come to think of it, there's some girls that play the piano at High School Commence-ment; but they ain't happy about it. No, ma'am, there isn't much culture; but maybe this is the place to tell
15 you that we've got a lot of pleasures of a kind here: we like the sun comin' up over the mountain in the morning, and we all notice a good deal about the birds. We pay a lot of attention to them. And we watch the change of the seasons; yes, everybody
20 knows about them. But those other things – you're right, ma'am, – there ain't much. – *Robinson Crusoe* and the Bible; and Handel's "Largo", we all know that; and Whistler's "Mother" – those are just about as far as we go.

25 LADY IN A BOX. So I thought. Thank you, Mr. Webb.

STAGE MANAGER. Thank you, Mr. Webb.

(Mr. Webb retires.)

---

1 **I dunno:** *I don't know.*
2 **diligent:** fleißig, emsig.
6 **to leave alone:** in Ruhe lassen.
12 f. **High School Commencement:** Schulabschlußfeier, Zeugnisvertei-lung.
23 **Whistler:** James McNeal W. (1834–1903), amerikanischer Maler.

Now, we'll go back to the town. It's early afternoon.
All 2,642 have had their dinners and all the dishes
have been washed.
(Mr. Webb, having removed his coat, returns and
5   *starts pushing a lawn mower to and fro beside his*
house.)
There's an early-afternoon calm in our town: a buz-
zin' and a hummin' from the school buildings; only a
few buggies on Main Street – the horses dozing at the
10   hitching posts; you all remember what it's like. Doc
Gibbs is in his office, tapping people and making
them say "ah". Mr. Webb's cuttin' his lawn over
there; one man in ten thinks it's a privilege to push his
own lawn mower.
15   No, sir. It's later than I thought. There are the
children coming home from school already.
(Shrill girls' voices are heard, off left. Emily comes
along Main Street, carrying some books. There are
some signs that she is imagining herself to be a lady of
20   *startling elegance.)*

EMILY. I *can't*, Lois. I've got to go home and help my
mother. I *promised*.

MR. WEBB. Emily, walk simply. Who do you think you
are today?

---

4 **to remove:** hier: ausziehen.
5 **lawn mower:** Rasenmäher.
   to and fro: hin und her.
7f. **to buzz:** summen, surren.
8 **to hum:** summen.
9 **buggy:** leichte Kutsche.
   to doze: dösen.
11 **to tap:** hier: abklopfen.
20 **startling:** aufsehenerregend.

EMILY. Papa, you're terrible. One minute you tell me to
   stand up straight and the next minute you call me
   names. I just don't listen to you.
   (She gives him an abrupt kiss.)
5 MR. WEBB. Golly, I never got a kiss from such a great
   lady before.
   *(He goes out of sight. Emily leans over and picks some
   flowers by the gate of her house.*
   George Gibbs comes careening down Main Street. He
10 *is throwing a ball up to dizzying heights, and waiting*
   to catch it again. This sometimes requires his taking six
   steps backward. He bumps into an old lady invisible
   to us.)
   GEORGE. Excuse me, Mrs. Forrest.
15 STAGE MANAGER *(as Mrs. Forrest).* Go out and play in
   the fields, young man. You got no business playing
   baseball on Main Street.
   GEORGE. Awfully sorry, Mrs. Forrest. – Hello, Emily.
   EMILY. H'lo.
20 GEORGE. You made a fine speech in class.
   EMILY. Well . . . I was really ready to make a speech
   about the Monroe Doctrine, but at the last minute
   Miss Corcoran made me talk about the Louisiana

2f. **to call s.o. names:** jdn. beschimpfen.
4 **abrupt:** unvermittelt, abrupt.
5 **golly:** Menschenskind, Donnerwetter.
9 **to career:** gehen mit Hüpfern nach rechts und links.
10 **dizzying:** schwindelerregend.
12 **to bump into:** zusammenstoßen mit.
16 **you got no business:** *you have got no business:* es gehört sich nicht,
   du darfst nicht.
22 **Monroe Doctrine:** von Präsident James Monroe 1823 dargelegte
   Prinzipien der amerikanischen Außenpolitik, basierend auf der poli-
   tischen Trennung von Alter und Neuer Welt.

Purchase instead. I worked an awful long time on
both of them.

GEORGE. Gee, it's funny, Emily. From my window up
there I can just see your head nights when you're
doing your homework over in your room.

EMILY. Why, can you?

GEORGE. You certainly do stick to it, Emily. I don't see
how you can sit still that long. I guess you like school.

EMILY. Well, I always feel it's something you have to go
through.

GEORGE. Yeah.

EMILY. I don't mind it really. It passes the time.

GEORGE. Yeah. – Emily, what do you think? We might
work out a kinda telegraph from your window to
mine; and once in a while you could give me a kinda
hint or two about one of those algebra problems. I
don't mean the answers, Emily, of course not . . . just
some little hint . . .

EMILY. Oh, I think *hints* are allowed. – So – ah – if you
get stuck, George, you whistle to me; and I'll give
you some hints.

GEORGE. Emily, you're just naturally bright, I guess.

EMILY. I figure that it's just the way a person's born.

GEORGE. Yeah. But, you see, I want to be a farmer, and

1 **purchase:** Kauf, Erwerbung; *Louisiana Purchase* bezieht sich auf
  den größten Landerwerb in der amerikanischen Geschichte, den
  Ankauf des westlich des Mississippi gelegenen Teils der französi-
  schen Kolonie Louisiane von 1803.
3 **gee:** Mensch, Donnerwetter, meine Güte.
4 **nights:** häufig nachts.
7 **to stick to s.th.:** sich einer Sache (intensiv) widmen, dabeibleiben.
14 **kinda:** *kind of.*
16 **algebra problem:** Algebraaufgabe.
23 **I figure:** ich glaube, ich denke mir.

my Uncle Luke says whenever I'm ready I can come
over and work on his farm and if I'm any good I can
just gradually have it.

EMILY. You mean the house and everything?

5 *(Enter Mrs. Webb with a large bowl and sits on the
bench by her trellis.)*

GEORGE. Yeah. Well, thanks ... I better be getting out
to the baseball field. Thanks for the talk, Emily. –
Good afternoon, Mrs. Webb.

10 MRS. WEBB. Good afternoon, George.

GEORGE. So long, Emily.

EMILY. So long, George.

MRS. WEBB. Emily, come and help me string these beans
for the winter. George Gibbs let himself have a real
15 conversation, didn't he? Why, he's growing up. How
old would George be?

EMILY. I don't know.

MRS. WEBB. Let's see. He must be almost sixteen.

EMILY. Mama, I made a speech in class today and I was
20 very good.

MRS. WEBB. You must recite it to your father at supper.
What was it about?

EMILY. The Louisiana Purchase. It was like silk off a
spool. I'm going to make speeches all my life. –
25 Mama, are these big enough?

MRS. WEBB. Try and get them a little bigger if you can.

EMILY. Mama, will you answer me a question, serious?

MRS. WEBB. Seriously, dear – not serious.

EMILY. Seriously, – will you?

---

11 **So long:** Bis dann; Bis später.
21 **to recite:** aufsagen, vortragen.
24 **spool:** Spule.

MRS. WEBB. Of course, I will.

EMILY. Mama, am I good looking?

MRS. WEBB. Yes, of course you are. All my children have got good features; I'd be ashamed if they hadn't.

5 EMILY. Oh, Mama, that's not what I mean. What I mean is: am I *pretty*?

MRS. WEBB. I've already told you, yes. Now that's enough of that. You have a nice young pretty face. I never heard of such foolishness.

10 EMILY. Oh, Mama, you never tell us the truth about anything.

MRS. WEBB. I *am* telling you the truth.

EMILY. Mama, were *you* pretty?

MRS. WEBB. Yes, I was, if I do say it. I was the prettiest
15 girl in town next to Mamie Cartwright.

EMILY. But, Mama, you've got to say *some*thing about me. Am I pretty enough . . . to get anybody . . . to get people interested in me?

MRS. WEBB. Emily, you make me tired. Now stop it.
20 You're pretty enough for all normal purposes. – Come along now and bring that bowl with you.

EMILY. Oh, Mama, you're no help at all.

STAGE MANAGER. Thank you. Thank you! That'll do. We'll have to interrupt again here. Thank you, Mrs.
25 Webb; thank you, Emily.

(Mrs. Webb and Emily withdraw.)

There are some more things we want to explore about this town.

*(He comes to the center of the stage. During the
30 following speech the lights gradually dim to darkness, leaving only a spot on him.)*

---

30 **to dim:** sich verdunkeln.

I think this is a good time to tell you that the
Cartwright interests have just begun building a new
bank in Grover's Corners – had to go to Vermont for
the marble, sorry to say. And they've asked a friend
5   of mine what they should put in the cornerstone for
people to dig up . . . a thousand years from now. . . .
Of course, they've put in a copy of the *New York
Times* and a copy of Mr. Webb's *Sentinel*. . . . We're
kind of interested in this because some scientific fellas
10 have found a way of painting all that reading matter
with a glue – a silicate glue – that'll make it keep a
thousand – two thousand years.
We're putting in a Bible . . . and the Constitution of
the United States – and a copy of William Shake-
15 speare's plays. What do you say, folks? What do you
think?
Y'know – Babylon once had two million people in it,
and all we know about 'em is the names of the kings
and some copies of wheat contracts . . . and contracts
20 for the sale of slaves. Yet every night all those families
sat down to supper, and the father came home from his
work, and the smoke went up the chimney, – same as
here. And even in Greece and Rome, all we know
about the *real* life of the people is what we can piece
25 together out of the joking poems and the comedies
they wrote for the theatre back then.
So I'm going to have a copy of this play put in the

---

2 **interests** (pl.): hier: Konzern.
5 **cornerstone**: Grundstein.
11 **glue**: Klebstoff, Leim.
   silicate: Silikat (kieselsaures Salz).
24 f. **to piece together**: zusammensetzen, -reimen.
26 **back then**: damals.

cornerstone and the people a thousand years from
now'll know a few simple facts about us – more than
the Treaty of Versailles and the Lindbergh flight.
See what I mean?

5   So – people a thousand years from now – this is the
way we were in the provinces north of New York at
the beginning of the twentieth century. – This is the
way we were: in our growing up and in our marrying
and in our living and in our dying.

10   *(A choir partially concealed in the orchestra pit has*
begun singing "Blessed Be the Tie That Binds".
Simon Stimson stands directing them.
Two ladders have been pushed onto the stage; they
serve as indication of the second story in the Gibbs and
15   *Webb houses. George and Emily mount them, and*
apply themselves to their schoolwork.
Dr. Gibbs has entered and is seated in his kitchen
reading.)
Well! – good deal of time's gone by. It's evening.
20   You can hear choir practice going on in the Congregational Church.
The children are at home doing their schoolwork.
The day's running down like a tired clock.

---

3 **Treaty of Versailles:** Vertrag von Versailles (1918/19), der den
Ersten Weltkrieg beendete.
Lindbergh flight: erste Überquerung des Atlantik mit dem Flugzeug
(1927) durch Charles A. Lindbergh.
6 **provinces:** Gebiet, Gegend.
10 **partially** (adv.): teilweise.
orchestra pit: Orchestergraben.
12 **to direct:** hier: dirigieren.
14 **indication:** Hinweis, Andeutung.
16 **to apply o.s. to:** sich widmen, sich beschäftigen mit.
23 **to run down:** ablaufen.

SIMON STIMSON. Now look here, everybody. Music come
into the world to give pleasure. – Softer! Softer! Get
it out of your heads that music's only good when it's
loud. You leave loudness to the Methodists. You
5 couldn't beat 'em, even if you wanted to. Now again.
Tenors!

GEORGE. Hssst! Emily!

EMILY. Hello.

GEORGE. Hello!

10 EMILY. I can't work at all. The moonlight's so *terrible*.

GEORGE. Emily, did you get the third problem?

EMILY. Which?

GEORGE. The *third*?

EMILY. Why, yes, George – that's the easiest of them all.

15 GEORGE. I don't see it. Emily, can you give me a hint?

EMILY. I'll tell you one thing: the answer's in yards.

GEORGE. !!! In yards? How do you mean?

EMILY. In *square* yards.

GEORGE. Oh . . . in square yards.

20 EMILY. Yes, George, don't you see?

GEORGE. Yeah.

EMILY. In square yards of *wallpaper*.

GEORGE. Wallpaper, – oh, I see. Thanks a lot, Emily.

EMILY. You're welcome. My, isn't the moonlight *ter-*
25 *rible*? And choir practice going on. – I think if you
hold your breath you can hear the train all the way to
Contoocook. Hear it?

GEORGE. M-m-m – What do you know!

EMILY. Well, I guess I better go back and try to work.

---

6 **tenor:** Tenor.
22 **wallpaper:** Tapete.
24 **my:** hier: meine Güte; herrje.

GEORGE. Good night, Emily. And thanks.

EMILY. Good night, George.

SIMON STIMSON. Before I forget it: how many of you will
be able to come in Tuesday afternoon and sing at
5 Fred Hersey's wedding? – show your hands. That'll
be fine; that'll be right nice. We'll do the same music
we did for Jane Trowbridge's last month.
– Now we'll do: "Art Thou Weary; Art Thou Languid?" It's a question, ladies and gentlemen, make it
10 talk. Ready.

DR. GIBBS. Oh, George, can you come down a minute?

GEORGE. Yes, Pa.

(He descends the ladder.)

DR. GIBBS. Make yourself comfortable, George; I'll only
15 keep you a minute. George, how old are you?

GEORGE. I? I'm sixteen, almost seventeen.

DR. GIBBS. What do you want to do after school's over?

GEORGE. Why, you know, Pa. I want to be a farmer on
Uncle Luke's farm.

20 DR. GIBBS. You'll be willing, will you, to get up early and
milk and feed the stock . . . and you'll be able to hoe
and hay all day?

GEORGE. Sure, I will. What are you . . . what do you
mean, Pa?

25 DR. GIBBS. Well, George, while I was in my office today I
heard a funny sound . . . and what do you think it
was? It was your mother chopping wood. There you

---

8 **art thou** (arch./poet.): *are you.*
8f. **languid:** matt.
21 **stock:** Vieh.
   to hoe: hacken.
22 **to hay:** heuen.
27 **to chop:** (zer)hacken.

see your mother – getting up early; cooking meals all
day long; washing and ironing; – and still she has to
go out in the back yard and chop wood. I suppose she
just got tired of asking you. She just gave up and
decided it was easier to do it herself. And you eat her
meals, and put on the clothes she keeps nice for you,
and you run off and play baseball, – like she's some
hired girl we keep around the house but that we don't
like very much. Well, I knew all I had to do was call
your attention to it. Here's a handkerchief, son.
George, I've decided to raise your spending money
twenty-five cents a week. Not, of course, for chopping wood for your mother, because that's a present
you give her, but because you're getting older – and I
imagine there are lots of things you must find to do
with it.

GEORGE. Thanks, Pa.

DR. GIBBS. Let's see – tomorrow's your payday. You can
count on it – Hmm. Probably Rebecca'll feel she
ought to have some more too. Wonder what could
have happened to your mother. Choir practice never
was as late as this before.

GEORGE. It's only half past eight, Pa.

DR. GIBBS. I don't know why she's in that old choir. She
hasn't any more voice than an old crow. . . . Traipsin'
around the streets at this hour of the night . . . Just
about time you retired, don't you think?

GEORGE. Yes, Pa.

(*George mounts to his place on the ladder. Laughter
and good nights can be heard on stage left and presently Mrs. Gibbs, Mrs. Soames and Mrs. Webb come*

25 **crow:** Krähe.

*down Main Street. When they arrive at the corner of
the stage they stop.)*

MRS. SOAMES. Good night, Martha. Good night, Mr.
Foster.

5 MRS. WEBB. I'll tell Mr. Webb; I *know* he'll want to put it
in the paper.

MRS. GIBBS. My, it's late!

MRS. SOAMES. Good night, Irma.

MRS. GIBBS. Real nice choir practice, wa'n't it? Myrtle
10 Webb! Look at that moon, will you! Tsk-tsk-tsk.
Potato weather, for sure.

(They are silent a moment, gazing up at the moon.)

MRS. SOAMES. Naturally I didn't want to say a word about
it in front of those others, but now we're alone –
15 really, it's the worst scandal that ever was in this
town!

MRS. GIBBS. What?

MRS. SOAMES. Simon Stimson!

MRS. GIBBS. Now, Louella!

20 MRS. SOAMES. But, Julia! To have the organist of a
church *drink* and *drunk* year after year. You know he
was drunk tonight.

MRS. GIBBS. Now, Louella! We all know about Mr.
Stimson, and we all know about the troubles he's
25 been through, and Dr. Ferguson knows too, and if
Dr. Ferguson keeps him on there in his job the only
thing the rest of us can do is just not to notice it.

MRS. SOAMES. *Not to notice it!* But it's getting worse.

MRS. WEBB. No, it isn't, Louella. It's getting better. I've
30 been in that choir twice as long as you have. It doesn't
happen anywhere near so often. . . . My, I hate to go

---

30 f. **not anywhere near so:** nicht annähernd so.

to bed on a night like this. – I better hurry. Those
children'll be sitting up till all hours. Good night,
Louella.
(They all exchange good nights. She hurries down-
5   *stage, enters her house and disappears.)*
MRS. GIBBS. Can you get home safe, Louella?
MRS. SOAMES. It's as bright as day. I can see Mr. Soames
scowling at the window now. You'd think we'd been
to a dance the way the menfolk carry on.
10   *(More good nights. Mrs. Gibbs arrives at her home*
and passes through the trellis into the kitchen.)
MRS. GIBBS. Well, we had a real good time.
DR. GIBBS. You're late enough.
MRS. GIBBS. Why, Frank, it ain't any later 'n usual.
15   DR. GIBBS. And you stopping at the corner to gossip with
a lot of hens.
MRS. GIBBS. Now, Frank, don't be grouchy. Come out
and smell the heliotrope in the moonlight.
(They stroll out arm in arm along the footlights.)
20   Isn't that wonderful? What did you do all the time I
was away?
DR. GIBBS. Oh, I read – as usual. What were the girls
gossiping about tonight?
MRS. GIBBS. Well, believe me, Frank – there is something
25   to gossip about.

---

2 **till all hours:** bis spät in die Nacht hinein.
8 **to scowl:** finster blicken.
9 **menfolk:** Mannsleute.
   to carry on: hier: sich anstellen, sich (übertrieben) aufführen.
12 **to have a good time:** Spaß haben, sich gut unterhalten.
15 **to gossip:** klatschen, tratschen.
17 **grouchy:** griesgrämig, mürrisch.
19 **to stroll:** schlendern, spazierengehen.

DR. GIBBS. Hmm! Simon Stimson far gone, was he?

MRS. GIBBS. Worst I've ever seen him. How'll that end, Frank? Dr. Ferguson can't forgive him forever.

DR. GIBBS. I guess I know more about Simon Stimson's
5 affairs than anybody in this town. Some people ain't made for small-town life. I don't know how that'll end; but there's nothing we can do but just leave it alone. Come, get in.

MRS. GIBBS. No, not yet ... Frank, I'm worried about
10 you.

DR. GIBBS. What are you worried about?

MRS. GIBBS. I think it's my duty to make plans for you to get a real rest and change. And if I get that legacy, well, I'm going to insist on it.

15 DR. GIBBS. Now, Julia, there's no sense in going over that again.

MRS. GIBBS. Frank, you're just *unreasonable*!

DR. GIBBS (*starting into the house*). Come on, Julia, it's getting late. First thing you know you'll catch cold. I
20 gave George a piece of my mind tonight. I reckon you'll have your wood chopped for a while anyway. No, no, start getting upstairs.

MRS. GIBBS. Oh, dear. There's always so many things to pick up, seems like. You know, Frank, Mrs. Fairchild
25 always locks her front door every night. All those people up that part of town do.

DR. GIBBS (*blowing out the lamp*). They're all getting

---

1 **far gone:** fortgeschritten; (fig.) ‚hinüber‘, sehr betrunken.
15 **to go over s.th.:** etwas durchgehen, überdenken.
20 **to give s.o. a piece of one's mind:** schimpfen, jdm. seine Meinung sagen.
   I reckon: ich glaube, meine (AE).

citified, that's the trouble with them. They haven't got nothing fit to burgle and everybody knows it.
(They disappear.
Rebecca climbs up the ladder beside George.)

5 GEORGE. Get out, Rebecca. There's only room for one at this window. You're always spoiling everything.

REBECCA. Well, let me look just a minute.

GEORGE. Use your own window.

REBECCA. I did, but there's no moon there. . . . George,
10 do you know what I think, do you? I think maybe the moon's getting nearer and nearer and there'll be a big 'splosion.

GEORGE. Rebecca, you don't know anything. If the moon were getting nearer, the guys that sit up all
15 night with telescopes would see it first and they'd tell about it, and it'd be in all the newspapers.

REBECCA. George, is the moon shining on South America, Canada and half the whole world?

GEORGE. Well – prob'ly is.
20 *(The stage manager strolls on.*
Pause. The sound of crickets is heard.)

STAGE MANAGER. Nine thirty. Most of the lights are out. No, there's Constable Warren trying a few doors on Main Street. And here comes Editor Webb, after
25 putting his newspaper to bed.
(Mr. Warren, an elderly policeman, comes along Main Street from the right, Mr. Webb from the left.)

MR. WEBB. Good evening, Bill.

---

1 **citified:** verstädtert.
2 **to burgle:** (bei einem Einbruch) stehlen.
14 **guy:** Mann, Kerl (AE).
15 **telescope:** Fernrohr, Teleskop.
21 **cricket:** Grille.

CONSTABLE WARREN. Evenin', Mr. Webb.

MR. WEBB. Quite a moon!

CONSTABLE WARREN. Yepp.

MR. WEBB. All quiet tonight?

5 CONSTABLE WARREN. Simon Stimson is rollin' around a little. Just saw his wife movin' out to hunt for him so I looked the other way – there he is now.
(Simon Stimson comes down Main Street from the left, only a trace of unsteadiness in his walk.)

10 MR. WEBB. Good evening, Simon ... Town seems to have settled down for the night pretty well. ...
(Simon Stimson comes up to him and pauses a moment and stares at him, swaying slightly.)
Good evening ... Yes, most of the town's settled
15 down for the night, Simon. ... I guess we better do the same. Can I walk along a ways with you?
(Simon Stimson continues on his way without a word and disappears at the right.)
Good night.

20 CONSTABLE WARREN. I don't know how that's goin' to end, Mr. Webb.

MR. WEBB. Well, he's seen a peck of trouble, one thing after another. ... Oh, Bill ... if you see my boy smoking cigarettes, just give him a word, will you?
25 He thinks a lot of you, Bill.

CONSTABLE WARREN. I don't think he smokes no ciga-

---

5 **to roll:** hier: torkeln.
9 **unsteadiness:** Unsicherheit, Schwanken.
13 **to sway:** schwanken, taumeln.
16 **ways** (AE): *way*.
22 **a peck:** eine Menge.
24 **to give s.o. a word:** ein paar Worte sagen, jdn. auf etwas ansprechen.

rettes, Mr. Webb. Leastways, not more'n two or three a year.

MR. WEBB. Hm . . . I hope not. – Well, good night, Bill.

CONSTABLE WARREN. Good night, Mr. Webb.

5 *(Exit.)*

MR. WEBB. Who's that up there? Is that you, Myrtle?

EMILY. No, it's me, Papa.

MR. WEBB. Why aren't you in bed?

EMILY. I don't know. I just can't sleep yet, Papa. The

10 moonlight's so *won*-derful. And the smell of Mrs. Gibbs' heliotrope. Can you smell it?

MR. WEBB. Hm . . . Yes. Haven't any troubles on your mind, have you, Emily?

EMILY. *Troubles*, Papa? *No.*

15 MR. WEBB. Well, enjoy yourself, but don't let your mother catch you. Good night, Emily.

EMILY. Good night, Papa.

(Mr. Webb crosses into the house, whistling "Blessed Be the Tie That Binds" and disappears.)

20 REBECCA. I never told you about that letter Jane Crofut got from her minister when she was sick. He wrote Jane a letter and on the envelope the address was like this: It said: <u>Jane Crofut</u>; <u>The Crofut Farm</u>; <u>Grover's Corners</u>; <u>Sutton County</u>; <u>New Hampshire</u>; <u>United</u>

25 <u>States of America</u>.

GEORGE. What's funny about that?

REBECCA. But listen, it's not finished: the United States of America; <u>Continent of North America</u>; <u>Western Hemisphere</u>; the <u>Earth</u>; the <u>Solar System</u>; the <u>Uni-</u>

---

1 **leastways:** *at least.*
21 **minister:** hier: (freikirchlicher) Geistlicher.

verse; <u>the Mind of God</u> – that's what it said on the envelope.

GEORGE. What do you know!

REBECCA. And the postman brought it just the same.

5 GEORGE. What do you know!

STAGE MANAGER. That's the end of the First Act, friends. You can go and smoke now, those that smoke.

Thomas Foley
54 Magnolia Dr.
Rocky Point
Suffolk County
New York, 11778
U.S.A.
Continent of North Am.
Western Hemisphere
the Earth
the Solar System
the Universe
the Mind of God

Act II

The tables and chairs of the two kitchens are still on the
stage.
The ladders and the small bench have been withdrawn.
5 *The stage manager has been at his accustomed place*
watching the audience return to its seats.

STAGE MANAGER. Three years have gone by.
　　Yes, the sun's come up over a thousand times.
　　Summers and winters have cracked the mountains a
10　little bit more and the rains have brought down some
　　of the dirt.
　　Some babies that weren't even born before have
　　begun talking regular sentences already; and a
　　number of people who thought they were right young
15　and spry have noticed that they can't bound up a
　　flight of stairs like they used to, without their heart
　　fluttering a little.
　　All that can happen in a thousand days.
　　Nature's been pushing and contriving in other ways,
20　too: a number of young people fell in love and got
　　married.

---

　9 **to crack:** spalten.
　15 **spry:** flink, aktiv.
　　　to bound up: heraufspringen, -hüpfen.
　17 **to flutter:** hier: klopfen.
　19 **pushing:** rührig.
　　　contriving: erfinderisch, erfolgreich tätig.

Yes, the mountain got bit away a few fractions of an
inch; millions of gallons of water went by the mill;
and here and there a new home was set up under a
roof.

5   Almost everybody in the world gets married, – you
know what I mean? In our town there aren't hardly
any exceptions. Most everybody in the world climbs
into their graves married.

The First Act was called the Daily Life. This act is
10   called Love and Marriage. There's another act coming after this: I reckon you can guess what that's
about.

So:

It's three years later. It's 1904.

15   It's July 7th, just after High School Commencement.
That's the time most of our young people jump up
and get married.

Soon as they've passed their last examinations in solid
geometry and Cicero's Orations, looks like they sud-
20   denly feel themselves fit to be married.

It's early morning. Only this time it's been raining.
It's been pouring and thundering.

Mrs. Gibbs' garden, and Mrs. Webb's here: drenched.
All those bean poles and pea vines: drenched.

---

1 **fraction:** Bruchteil.
2 **gallon:** Gallone (amerikanisches Hohlmaß, 3,78 l).
16 f. **to jump up and do s.th.:** (plötzlich) anfangen, etwas zu tun.
18 f. **solid geometry:** Stereometrie (Lehre von den geometrischen Kör-
pern).
19 **oration:** Rede.
23 **drenched:** durchnäßt, aufgeweicht.
24 **pole:** Pfahl, Stange.
vine: rankende Pflanze, Ranke.

All yesterday over there on Main Street, the rain
looked like curtains being blown along.
Hm . . . it may begin again any minute.
There! You can hear the 5:45 for Boston.

5 (*Mrs. Gibbs and Mrs. Webb enter their kitchen and
start the day as in the First Act.*)
And there's Mrs. Gibbs and Mrs. Webb come down
to make breakfast, just as though it were an ordinary
day. I don't have to point out to the women in my

10 audience that those ladies they see before them, both
of those ladies cooked three meals a day – one of 'em
for twenty years, the other for forty – and no summer
vacation. They brought up two children apiece,
washed, cleaned the house, – and *never a nervous*

15 *breakdown*.
It's like what one of those Middle West poets said:
You've got to love life to have life, and you've got to
have life to love life. . . . It's what they call a vicious
circle.

20 HOWIE NEWSOME (*off stage left*). Giddap, Bessie!
STAGE MANAGER. Here comes Howie Newsome delivering the milk. And there's Si Crowell delivering the
papers like his brother before him.
(*Si Crowell has entered hurling imaginary newspapers

25 into doorways; Howie Newsome has come along Main
Street with Bessie.*)
SI CROWELL. Morning, Howie.
HOWIE NEWSOME. Morning, Si. – Anything in the papers
I ought to know?

---

13 **vacation:** Urlaub.
   apiece: je.
14 f. **nervous breakdown:** Nervenzusammenbruch.
18 f. **vicious circle:** Teufelskreis.

SI CROWELL. Nothing much, except we're losing about
   the best baseball pitcher Grover's Corners ever had –
   George Gibbs.

HOWIE NEWSOME. Reckon he is.

5 SI CROWELL. He could hit and run bases, too.

HOWIE NEWSOME. Yep. Mighty fine ball player. – Whoa!
   Bessie! I guess I can stop and talk if I've a mind to!

SI CROWELL. I don't see how he could give up a thing like
   that just to get married. Would you, Howie?

10 HOWIE NEWSOME. Can't tell, Si. Never had no talent that
   way.

   (Constable Warren enters. They exchange good morn-
   ings.)

   You're up early, Bill.

15 CONSTABLE WARREN. Seein' if there's anything I can do
   to prevent a flood. River's been risin' all night.

HOWIE NEWSOME. Si Crowell's all worked up here about
   George Gibbs' retiring from baseball.

CONSTABLE WARREN. Yes, sir; that's the way it goes.

20   Back in '84 we had a player, Si – even George Gibbs
   couldn't touch him. Name of Hank Todd. Went down
   to Maine and become a parson. Wonderful ball
   player. – Howie, how does the weather look to you?

HOWIE NEWSOME. Oh, 'tain't bad. Think maybe it'll clear

25   up for good.

   (Constable Warren and Si Crowell continue on their
   way.

---

2 **pitcher:** Feldspieler beim Baseball, der die Bälle wirft.
5 **base:** Mal (auf dem Baseballfeld).
7 **to have a mind to s.th.:** zu etwas Lust haben.
10 **talent:** Begabung, Talent.
17 **worked up:** aufgeregt, aufgebracht.
21 **to touch:** hier: heranreichen an.
25 **for good:** endgültig.

Howie Newsome brings the milk first to Mrs. Gibbs'
house. She meets him by the trellis.)

MRS. GIBBS. Good morning, Howie. Do you think it's
going to rain again?

5 HOWIE NEWSOME. Morning, Mrs. Gibbs. It rained so
heavy, I think maybe it'll clear up.

MRS. GIBBS. Certainly hope it will.

HOWIE NEWSOME. How much did you want today?

MRS. GIBBS. I'm going to have a houseful of relations,
10   Howie. Looks to me like I'll need three-a-milk and
two-a-cream.

HOWIE NEWSOME. My wife says to tell you we both hope
they'll be very happy, Mrs. Gibbs. Know they *will*.

MRS. GIBBS. Thanks a lot, Howie. Tell your wife I hope
15   she gits there to the wedding.

HOWIE NEWSOME. Yes, she'll be there; she'll be there if
she kin.

(Howie Newsome crosses to Mrs. Webb's house.)
Morning, Mrs. Webb.

20 MRS. WEBB. Oh, good morning, Mr. Newsome. I told you
four quarts of milk, but I hope you can spare me
another.

HOWIE NEWSOME. Yes'm . . . and the two of cream.

MRS. WEBB. Will it start raining again, Mr. Newsome?

25 HOWIE NEWSOME. Well. Just sayin' to Mrs. Gibbs as how
it may lighten up. Mrs. Newsome told me to tell you
as how we hope they'll both be very happy, Mrs.
Webb. Know they *will*.

MRS. WEBB. Thank you, and thank Mrs. Newsome and
30   we're counting on seeing you at the wedding.

---

10 **three-a-milk:** *three (quarts) of milk.*
17 **kin:** *can.*

HOWIE NEWSOME. Yes, Mrs. Webb. We hope to git there. Couldn't miss that. Come on, Bessie.

(Exit Howie Newsome.

Dr. Gibbs descends in shirt sleeves, and sits down at his breakfast table.)

DR. GIBBS. Well, Ma, the day has come. You're losin' one of your chicks.

MRS. GIBBS. Frank Gibbs, don't you say another word. I feel like crying every minute. Sit down and drink your coffee.

DR. GIBBS. The groom's up shaving himself – only there ain't an awful lot to shave. Whistling and singing, like he's glad to leave us. – Every now and then he says "I do" to the mirror, but it don't sound convincing to me.

MRS. GIBBS. I declare, Frank, I don't know how he'll get along. I've arranged his clothes and seen to it he's put warm things on, – Frank! they're too *young*. Emily won't think of such things. He'll catch his death of cold within a week.

DR. GIBBS. I was remembering my wedding morning, Julia.

MRS. GIBBS. Now don't start that, Frank Gibbs.

DR. GIBBS. I was the scaredest young fella in the State of New Hampshire. I thought I'd make a mistake for sure. And when I saw you comin' down that aisle I thought you were the prettiest girl I'd ever seen, but the only trouble was that I'd never seen you before.

---

11 **groom:** Bräutigam.
17 **to see to:** dafür sorgen.
19f. **to catch one's death of cold:** sich zu Tode erkälten.
24 **scared:** erschrocken, verschreckt.
26 **aisle:** Kirchenschiff, Mittelgang.

        There I was in the Congregational Church marryin' a
        total stranger.

MRS. GIBBS. And how do you think I felt! – Frank,
        weddings are perfectly awful things. Farces, – that's
5   what they are!

        (She puts a plate before him.)

        Here, I've made something for you.

DR. GIBBS. Why, Julia Hersey – French toast!

MRS. GIBBS. 'Tain't hard to make and I had to do *some-*
10 *thing.*

        (Pause. Dr. Gibbs pours on the syrup.)

DR. GIBBS. How'd you sleep last night, Julia?

MRS. GIBBS. Well, I heard a lot of the hours struck
        off.

15 DR. GIBBS. Ye-e-s! I get a shock every time I think of
        George setting out to be a family man – that great
        gangling thing! – I tell you Julia, there's nothing so
        terrifying in the world as a *son*. The relation of father
        and son is the darndest, awkwardest –

20 MRS. GIBBS. Well, mother and daughter's no picnic, let
        me tell you.

DR. GIBBS. They'll have a lot of troubles, I suppose, but
        that's none of our business. Everybody has a right to
        their own troubles.

---

  4 **farce:** Posse, Farce.
  8 **French toast:** in Ei und Milch gebackene Brotscheibe.
  9 **'tain't:** *it isn't.*
 11 **syrup:** Sirup.
 17 **gangling:** hochgewachsen, schlaksig.
 18 **terrifying:** erschreckend, beängstigend.
 19 **darndest:** von *darned* (slang für *damned*) ›verflixt‹.
     awkward: heikel, unbequem.
 20 **no picnic:** hier: nicht einfach, keine leichte Sache.

MRS. GIBBS *(at the table, drinking her coffee, medita-tively).* Yes ... people are meant to go through life two by two. 'Tain't natural to be lonesome.
(Pause. Dr. Gibbs starts laughing.)

5 DR. GIBBS. Julia, do you know one of the things I was scared of when I married you?

MRS. GIBBS. Oh, go along with you!

DR. GIBBS. I was afraid we wouldn't have material for conversation more'n'd last us a few weeks.

10 *(Both laugh.)*

I was afraid we'd run out and eat our meals in silence, that's a fact. – Well, you and I been conversing for twenty years now without any noticeable barren spells.

15 MRS. GIBBS. Well, – good weather, bad weather – 'tain't very choice, but I always find something to say.
(She goes to the foot of the stairs.)
Did you hear Rebecca stirring around upstairs?

DR. GIBBS. No. Only day of the year Rebecca hasn't been
20 managing everybody's business up there. She's hiding in her room. – I got the impression she's crying.

MRS. GIBBS. Lord's sakes! – This has got to stop. – Rebecca! Rebecca! Come and get your breakfast.

---

1 f. **meditatively** (adv.): nachdenklich.
3 **lonesome:** einsam, allein.
7 **go along with you!:** hier: hör auf!
9 **more'n'd:** *more than would.*
11 **to run out** (*of s.th.*): ausgehen, knapp werden (*I have run out of s.th.:* mir ist etwas ausgegangen).
13 **barren:** leer, öde.
14 **spell:** (kurze) Zeitspanne.
16 **choice:** erlesen, ausgewählt.
22 **Lord's sakes!:** *For the Lord's sake!:* Um Gottes willen!

(George comes rattling down the stairs, very brisk.)

GEORGE. Good morning, everybody. Only five more
hours to live.

(Makes the gesture of cutting his throat, and a loud
5   *"k-k-k", and starts through the trellis.)*

MRS. GIBBS. George Gibbs, where are you going?

GEORGE. Just stepping across the grass to see my girl.

MRS. GIBBS. Now, George! You put on your overshoes.
It's raining torrents. You don't go out of this house

10   without you're prepared for it.

GEORGE. Aw, Ma. It's just a *step*!

MRS. GIBBS. George! You'll catch your death of cold and
cough all through the service.

DR. GIBBS. George, do as your mother tells you!

15   *(Dr. Gibbs goes upstairs.*
George returns reluctantly to the kitchen and pan-
tomimes putting on overshoes.)

MRS. GIBBS. From tomorrow on you can kill yourself in
all weathers, but while you're in my house you'll live

20   wisely, thank you. – Maybe Mrs. Webb isn't used to
callers at seven in the morning. – Here, take a cup of
coffee first.

GEORGE. Be back in a minute.

(He crosses the stage, leaping over the puddles.)

25   Good morning, Mother Webb.

MRS. WEBB. Goodness! You frightened me! – Now,
George, you can come in a minute out of the wet, but
you know I can't ask you in.

---

4 **gesture:** Geste, Gebärde.
9 **torrent:** Gießbach, Strom.
16 **reluctantly** (adv.): widerstrebend, widerwillig.
21 **caller:** Besucher.
24 **puddle:** Pfütze.

GEORGE. Why not –?

MRS. WEBB. George, you know's well as I do: the groom can't see his bride on his wedding day, not until he sees her in church.

5 GEORGE. Aw! – that's just a superstition. – Good morning, Mr. Webb.

(Enter Mr. Webb.)

MR. WEBB. Good morning, George.

GEORGE. Mr. Webb, you don't believe in that superstition, do you?

MR. WEBB. There's a lot of common sense in some superstitions, George.

(He sits at the table, facing right.)

MRS. WEBB. Millions have folla'd it, George, and you don't want to be the first to fly in the face of custom.

GEORGE. How is Emily?

MRS. WEBB. She hasn't waked up yet. I haven't heard a sound out of her.

20 GEORGE. Emily's *asleep*!!!

MRS. WEBB. No wonder! We were up 'til all hours, sewing and packing. Now I'll tell you what I'll do; you set down here a minute with Mr. Webb and drink this cup of coffee; and I'll go upstairs and see she doesn't come down and surprise you. There's some bacon, too; but don't be long about it.

(Exit Mrs. Webb.
Embarrassed silence.

---

5 **superstition:** Aberglaube.
11 **common sense:** gesunder Menschenverstand.
15 **to fly in the face of:** herausfordern.
28 **embarrassed:** verwirrt, verlegen.

Mr. Webb dunks doughnuts in his coffee.
More silence.)

MR. WEBB *(suddenly and loudly)*. Well, George, how are
you?

5 GEORGE *(startled, choking over his coffee)*. Oh, fine, I'm
fine.

(Pause.)

Mr. Webb, what sense could there be in a superstition like that?

10 MR. WEBB. Well, you see, – on her wedding morning a
girl's head's apt to be full of . . . clothes and one thing
and another. Don't you think that's probably it?

GEORGE. Ye-e-s. I never thought of that.

MR. WEBB. A girl's apt to be a mite nervous on her
15 wedding day.

(Pause.)

GEORGE. I wish a fellow could get married without all
that marching up and down.

MR. WEBB. Every man that's ever lived has felt that way
20 about it, George; but is hasn't been any use. It's the
womenfolk who've built up weddings, my boy. For
a while now the women have it all their own. A
man looks pretty small at a wedding, George. All
those good women standing shoulder to shoulder
25 making sure that the knot's tied in a mighty public
way.

GEORGE. But . . . you *believe* in it, don't you, Mr.
Webb?

---

1 **to dunk:** stippen, tunken.
   doughnut: (amerikanischer Frühstücks-)Krapfen, Berliner.
11 **is apt to be:** ist geneigt, . . . zu sein, ist wahrscheinlich.
14 **a mite:** ein kleines bißchen.
22 **to have it one's own:** etwas bestimmen, nach seinem Willen tun.

MR. WEBB *(with alacrity)*. Oh, yes; *oh, yes*. Don't you
misunderstand me, my boy. Marriage is a wonderful
thing, – wonderful thing. And don't you forget that,
George.

5 GEORGE. No, sir. – Mr. Webb, how old were you when
you got married?

MR. WEBB. Well, you see: I'd been to college and I'd
taken a little time to get settled. But Mrs. Webb – she
wasn't much older than what Emily is. Oh, age hasn't
10 much to do with it, George, – not compared with . . .
uh . . . other things.

GEORGE. What were you going to say, Mr. Webb?

MR. WEBB. Oh, I don't know. – Was I going to say
something?

15 *(Pause.)*
George, I was thinking the other night of some advice
my father gave me when I got married. Charles, he
said, Charles, start out early showing who's boss, he
said. Best thing to do is to give an order, even if it
20 don't make sense; just so she'll learn to obey. And he
said: if anything about your wife irritates you – her
conversation, or anything – just get up and leave the
house. That'll make it clear to her, he said. And, oh,
yes! he said never, *never* let your wife know how how
25 much money you have, never.

GEORGE. Well, Mr. Webb . . . I don't think I could . . .

MR. WEBB. So I took the opposite of my father's advice
and I've been happy ever since. And let that be a
lesson to you, George, never to ask advice on per-
30 sonal matters. – George, are you going to raise
chickens on your farm?

---

1 **alacrity:** Lebhaftigkeit.

GEORGE. What?

MR. WEBB. Are you going to raise chickens on your farm?

GEORGE. Uncle Luke's never been much interested, but
I thought –

5 MR. WEBB. A book came into my office the other day,
George, on the Philo System of raising chickens. I
want you to read it. I'm thinking of beginning in a
small way in the back yard, and I'm going to put an
incubator in the cellar –

10 *(Enter Mrs. Webb.)*

MRS. WEBB. Charles, are you talking about that old
incubator again? I thought you two'd be talking about
things worth while.

MR. WEBB *(bitingly)*. Well, Myrtle, if you want to give
15 the boy some good advice, I'll go upstairs and leave
you alone with him.

MRS. WEBB *(pulling George up)*. George, Emily's got to
come downstairs and eat her breakfast. She sends you
her love but she doesn't want to lay eyes on you.
20 Good-by.

GEORGE. Good-by.

*(George crosses the stage to his own home, bewildered
and crestfallen. He slowly dodges a puddle and disappears into his house.)*

25 MR. WEBB. Myrtle, I guess you don't know about that
older superstition.

MRS. WEBB. What do you mean, Charles?

---

9 **incubator:** Brutapparat.
13 **worth while:** lohnend.
18 f. **to send one's love:** herzlich grüßen lassen.
19 **to lay eyes on:** zu Gesicht bekommen, sehen.
23 **crestfallen:** niedergeschlagen.
　　to dodge: umgehen, ausweichen.

MR. WEBB. Since the cave men: no bridegroom should
see his father-in-law on the day of the wedding, or
near it. Now remember that.
(Both leave the stage.)

5 STAGE MANAGER. Thank you very much, Mr. and Mrs.
Webb. – Now I have to interrupt again here. You see,
we want to know how all this began – this wedding,
this plan to spend a lifetime together. I'm awfully
interested in how big things like that begin.

10 You know how it is: you're twenty-one or twenty-two
and you make some decisions; then whisssh! you're
seventy: you've been a lawyer for fifty years, and that
white-haired lady at your side has eaten over fifty
thousand meals with you.

15 How do such things begin?
George and Emily are going to show you now the
conversation they had when they first knew that . . .
that . . . as the saying goes . . . they were meant for
one another.

20 But before they do it I want you to try and remember
what it was like to have been very young.
And particularly the days when you were first in love;
when you were like a person sleepwalking, and you
didn't quite see the street you were in, and didn't

25 quite hear everything that was said to you.
You're just a little bit crazy. Will you remember that,
please?
Now they'll be coming out of high school at three
o'clock. George has just been elected President of the

30 Junior Class, and as it's June, that means he'll be
President of the Senior Class all next year. And

---

12 **lawyer:** Rechtsanwalt, Jurist.

Emily's just been elected Secretary and Treasurer. I
don't have to tell you how important that is.
*(He places a board across the backs of two chairs,
which he takes from those at the Gibbs family's table.*
5   *He brings two high stools from the wings and places
them behind the board. Persons sitting on the stools
will be facing the audience. This is the counter of Mr.
Morgan's drugstore. The sounds of young people's
voices are heard off left.)*
10   Yepp, – there they are coming down Main Street
now.
*(Emily, carrying an armful of – imaginary – school-
books, comes along Main Street from the left.)*
EMILY. I can't, Louise. I've got to go home. Good-by.
15   Oh, Ernestine! Ernestine! Can you come over tonight
and do Latin? Isn't that Cicero the worst thing –! Tell
your mother you *have* to. G'by. G'by, Helen. G'by,
Fred.
(George, also carrying books, catches up with her.)
20   GEORGE. Can I carry your books home for you, Emily?
EMILY *(coolly)*. Why . . . uh . . . Thank you. It isn't far.
(She gives them to him.)
GEORGE. Excuse me a minute, Emily. – Say, Bob, if I'm
a little late, start practice anyway. And give Herb
25   some long high ones.
EMILY. Good-by, Lizzy.
GEORGE. Good-by, Lizzy. – I'm awfully glad you were
elected, too, Emily.

---

1 **treasurer:** Schatzmeister.
5 **stool:** Hocker, Schemel.
  wings: hier: Kulissen.
19 **to catch up with s.o.:** jdn. einholen.
23 **say:** hier: ach, übrigens.

EMILY. Thank you.

(They have been standing on Main Street, almost against the back wall. They take the first steps toward the audience when George stops and says:)

5 GEORGE. Emily, why are you mad at me?

EMILY. I'm not mad at you.

GEORGE. You've been treating me so funny lately.

EMILY. Well, since you ask me, I might as well say it right out, George, –

10 *(She catches sight of a teacher passing.)*

Good-by, Miss Corcoran.

GEORGE. Good-by, Miss Corcoran. – Wha – what is it?

EMILY *(not scoldingly; finding it difficult to say)*. I don't like the whole change that's come over you in the last

15 year. I'm sorry if that hurts your feelings, but I've got to – tell the truth and shame the devil.

GEORGE. A *change*? Wha – what do you mean?

EMILY. Well, up to a year ago I used to like you a lot. And I used to watch you as you did everything . . .

20 because we'd been friends so long . . . and then you began spending all your time at *baseball* . . . and you never stopped to speak to anybody any more. Not even to your own family you didn't . . . and, George, it's a fact, you've got awful conceited and

25 stuck-up, and all the girls say so. They may not say so to your face, but that's what they say about you behind your back, and it hurts me to hear them say it, but I've got to agree with them a little. I'm sorry

---

5 **mad at:** böse, wütend auf.
7 **lately:** kürzlich, in letzter Zeit.
9 **right out:** unumwunden, frei heraus.
24 **conceited:** eingebildet.
25 **stuck-up:** hochnäsig, aufgeblasen.

if it hurts your feelings ... but I can't be sorry I
said it.

GEORGE. I ... I'm glad you said it, Emily. I never
thought that such a thing was happening to me. I
guess it's hard for a fella not to have faults creep into
his character.

*(They take a step or two in silence, then stand still in
misery.)*

EMILY. I always expect a man to be perfect and I think
he should be.

GEORGE. Oh ... I don't think it's possible to be perfect,
Emily.

EMILY. Well, my *father* is, and as far as I can see *your*
father is. There's no reason on earth why you
shouldn't be, too.

GEORGE. Well, I feel it's the other way round. That men
aren't naturally good; but girls are.

EMILY. Well, you might as well know right now that I'm
not perfect. It's not as easy for a girl to be perfect as a
man, because we girls are more – more – nervous. –
Now I'm sorry I said all that about you. I don't know
what made me say it.

GEORGE. Emily, –

EMILY. Now I can see it's not the truth at all. And I
suddenly feel that it isn't important, anyway.

GEORGE. Emily ... would you like an ice-cream soda, or
something, before you go home?

EMILY. Well, thank you. ... I would.

*(They advance toward the audience and make an
abrupt right turn, opening the door of Morgan's drug-*

---

26 **ice-cream soda:** Limonade mit Eiskrem.

*store. Under strong emotion, Emily keeps her face
down. George speaks to some passers-by.)*

GEORGE. Hello, Stew, – how are you? – Good afternoon, Mrs. Slocum.

5 *(The stage manager, wearing spectacles and assuming
the role of Mr. Morgan, enters abruptly from the right
and stands between the audience and the counter of his
soda fountain.)*

STAGE MANAGER. Hello, George. Hello, Emily. –
10 What'll you have? – Why, Emily Webb, – what you
been crying about?

GEORGE. *(He gropes for an explanation.)* She . . . she
just got an awful scare, Mr. Morgan. She almost got
run over by that hardware-store wagon. Everybody
15 says that Tom Huckins drives like a crazy man.

STAGE MANAGER *(drawing a drink of water)*. Well, now!
You take a drink of water, Emily. You look all shook
up. I tell you, you've got to look both ways before
you cross Main Street these days. Gets worse every
20 year. – What'll you have?

EMILY. I'll have a strawberry phosphate, thank you, Mr.
Morgan.

GEORGE. No, no, Emily. Have an ice-cream soda with
me. Two strawberry ice-cream sodas, Mr. Morgan.

25 STAGE MANAGER *(working the faucets)*. Two strawberry
ice-cream sodas, yes sir. Yes, sir. There are a
hundred and twenty-five horses in Grover's Corners
this minute I'm talking to you. State Inspector was in

---

8 **soda fountain:** Limonadeausschank.
12 **to grope for:** suchen nach, ringen um.
14 **hardware-store:** Eisenwarenhandlung.
25 **faucet:** Zapfhahn.

here yesterday. And now they're bringing in these
auto-mo-biles, the best thing to do is to just stay
home. Why, I can remember when a dog could go to
sleep all day in the middle of Main Street and nothing
5   come along to disturb him.
(He sets the imaginary glasses before them.)
There they are. Enjoy 'em.
(He sees a customer, right.)
Yes, Mrs. Ellis. What can I do for you?
10   *(He goes out right.)*
EMILY. They're so expensive.
GEORGE. No, no, – don't you think of that. We're celebrating our election. And then do you know what else
I'm celebrating?
15 EMILY. N-no.
GEORGE. I'm celebrating because I've got a friend who
tells me all the things that ought to be told me.
EMILY. George, *please* don't think of that. I don't know
why I said it. It's not true. You're –
20 GEORGE. No, Emily, you stick to it. I'm glad you spoke
to me like you did. But you'll *see*: I'm going to change
so quick – you bet I'm going to change. And, Emily, I
want to ask you a favor.
EMILY. What?
25 GEORGE. Emily, if I go away to State Agriculture College next year, will you write me a letter once in a
while?
EMILY. I certainly will. I certainly will, George . . .
(Pause. They start sipping the sodas through the straws.)

---

22 **you bet:** ganz bestimmt, du kannst dich darauf verlassen (*to bet:*
wetten).

26 f. **once in a while:** ab und zu.

29 **to sip:** nippen, schlürfen, langsam trinken.

It certainly seems like being away three years you'd
get out of touch with things. Maybe letters from
Grover's Corners wouldn't be so interesting after a
while. Grover's Corners isn't a very important place
5 when you think of all – New Hampshire; but I think
it's a very nice town.

GEORGE. The day wouldn't come when I wouldn't want
to know everything that's happening here. I know
that's true, Emily.

10 EMILY. Well, I'll try to make my letters interesting.
(Pause.)

GEORGE. Y'know. Emily, whenever I meet a farmer I
ask him if he thinks it's important to go to Agriculture
School to be a good farmer.

15 EMILY. Why, George –

GEORGE. Yeah, and some of them say that it's even a
waste of time. You can get all those things, anyway,
out of the pamphlets the government sends out. And
Uncle Luke's getting old, – he's about ready for me to
20 start in taking over his farm tomorrow, if I could.

EMILY. My!

GEORGE. And, like you say, being gone all that time . . .
in other places and meeting other people . . . Gosh, if
anything like that can happen I don't want to go
25 away. I guess new people aren't any better than old
ones. I'll bet they almost never are. Emily . . . I feel
that you're as good a friend as I've got. I don't need
to go and meet the people in other towns.

EMILY. But, George, maybe it's very important for you
30 to go and learn all that about – cattle judging and soils
and those things. . . . Of course, I don't know.

---

18 **pamphlet:** Broschüre.

GEORGE *(after a pause, very seriously)*. Emily, I'm going
to make up my mind right now. I won't go. I'll tell Pa
about it tonight.

EMILY. Why, George, I don't see why you have to decide
5 right now. It's a whole year away.

GEORGE. Emily, I'm glad you spoke to me about that . . .
that fault in my character. What you said was right;
but there was *one* thing wrong in it, and that was
when you said that for a year I wasn't noticing
10 people, and . . . you, for instance. Why, you say you
were watching me when I did everything . . . I was
doing the same about you all the time. Why, sure, – I
always thought about you as one of the chief people I
thought about. I always made sure where you were
15 sitting on the bleachers, and who you were with, and
for three days now I've been trying to walk home with
you; but something's always got in the way. Yesterday I was standing over against the wall waiting for
you, and you walked home with *Miss Corcoran*.

20 EMILY. George! . . . Life's awful funny! How could I
have known that? Why, I thought –

GEORGE. Listen, Emily, I'm going to tell you why I'm
not going to Agriculture School. I think that once
you've found a person that you're very fond of . . . I
25 mean a person who's fond of you, too, and likes you
enough to be interested in your character . . . Well, I
think that's just as important as college is, and even
more so. That's what I think.

EMILY. I think it's awfully important, too.

30 GEORGE. Emily.

EMILY. Y-yes, George.

15 **bleacher:** (billige) Sonnentribüne; von *to bleach* ›bleichen‹.

GEORGE. Emily, if I *do* improve and make a big change ... would you be ... I mean: *could* you be ...

EMILY. I ... I am now; I always have been.

GEORGE. *(Pause.)* So I guess this is an important talk we've been having.

EMILY. Yes ... yes.

GEORGE *(takes a deep breath and straightens his back).* Wait just a minute and I'll walk you home.
(With mounting alarm he digs into his pockets for the money.
The stage manager enters, right.
George, deeply embarrassed, but direct, says to him:) Mr. Morgan, I'll have to go home and get the money to pay you for this. It'll only take me a minute.

STAGE MANAGER *(pretending to be affronted).* What's that? George Gibbs, do you mean to tell me –!

GEORGE. Yes, but I had reasons, Mr. Morgan. – Look, here's my gold watch to keep until I come back with the money.

STAGE MANAGER. That's all right. Keep your watch. I'll trust you.

GEORGE. I'll be back in five minutes.

STAGE MANAGER. I'll trust you ten years, George, – not a day over. – Got all over your shock, Emily?

EMILY. Yes, thank you, Mr. Morgan. It was nothing.

GEORGE *(taking up the books from the counter).* I'm ready.
(They walk in grave silence across the stage and pass through the trellis at the Webbs' back door and disappear.

16 **affronted:** beleidigt.

*The stage manager watches them go out, then turns to
the audience, removing his spectacles.)*

STAGE MANAGER. Well, –

(He claps his hands as a signal.)

5   Now we're ready to get on with the wedding.

*(He stands waiting while the set is prepared for the next
scene.*

*Stagehands remove the chairs, tables and trellises from
the Gibbs and Webb houses.*

10   *They arrange the pews for the church in the center of
the stage. The congregation will sit facing the back
wall. The aisle of the church starts at the center of the
back wall and comes toward the audience.*

*A small platform is placed against the back wall on
15   which the stage manager will stand later, playing the
minister. The image of a stained-glass window is cast
from a lantern slide upon the back wall.*

*When all is ready the stage manager strolls to the center
of the stage, down front, and, musingly, addresses the
20   audience.)*

There are a lot of things to be said about a wedding;
there are a lot of thoughts that go on during a
wedding.

We can't get them all into one wedding, naturally,
25   and especially not into a wedding at Grover's Corners, where they're awfully plain and short.

---

6 **set:** hier: Bühnenbild.
8 **stagehand:** Bühnenarbeiter.
10 **pew:** Kirchenstuhl.
14 **platform:** Podium.
16 **stained-glass:** aus buntem Glas.
17 **lantern slide:** Dia, Lichtbild.
19 **musingly** (adv.): sinnend, nachdenklich.

In this wedding I play the minister. That gives me the
right to say a few more things about it.

For a while now, the play gets pretty serious.

Y'see, some churches say that marriage is a sacra-
ment. I don't quite know what that means, but I can
guess. Like Mrs. Gibbs said a few minutes ago:
People were made to live two-by-two.

This is a good wedding, but people are so put
together that even at a good wedding there's a lot of
confusion way down deep in people's minds and we
thought that that ought to be in our play, too.

The real hero of this scene isn't on the stage at all,
and you know who that is. It's like what one of those
European fellas said: every child born into the world
is nature's attempt to make a perfect human being.
Well, we've seen nature pushing and contriving for
some time now. We all know that nature's interested
in quantity; but I think she's interested in quality,
too, – that's why I'm in the ministry.

And don't forget all the other witnesses at this wedding, – the ancestors. Millions of them. Most of them
set out to live two-by-two, also. Millions of
them.

Well, that's all my sermon. 'Twan't very long,
anyway.

(The organ starts playing Handel's "Largo".
The congregation streams into the church and sits in
silence.
Church bells are heard.
Mrs. Gibbs sits in the front row, the first seat on the

21 **ancestor:** Vorfahre, Ahn.
24 **sermon:** Predigt.

aisle, the right section; next to her are Rebecca and Dr. Gibbs. Across the aisle Mrs. Webb, Wally and Mr. Webb. A small choir takes its place, facing the audience under the stained-glass window.

5   *Mrs. Webb, on the way to her place, turns back and speaks to the audience.)*

MRS. WEBB. I don't know why on earth I should be crying. I suppose there's nothing to cry about. It came over me at breakfast this morning; there was

10 Emily eating her breakfast as she's done for seventeen years and now she's going off to eat it in someone else's house. I suppose that's it.

And Emily! She suddenly said: I can't eat another mouthful, and she put her head down on the table

15 and *she* cried.

(She starts toward her seat in the church, but turns back and adds:)

Oh, I've got to say it: you know, there's something downright cruel about sending our girls out into

20 marriage this way.

I hope some of her girl friends have told her a thing or two. It's cruel, I know, but I couldn't bring myself to say anything. I went into it blind as a bat myself.

(In half-amused exasperation.)

25 The whole world's wrong, that's what's the matter. There they come.

(She hurries to her place in the pew.

George starts to come down the right aisle of the theatre, through the audience.

---

19 **downright:** geradezu.
23 **bat:** Fledermaus; *blind as a bat:* Redensart.
24 **exasperation:** Erbitterung.

Suddenly three members of his baseball team appear
by the right proscenium pillar and start whistling and
catcalling to him. They are dressed for the ball field.)

THE BASEBALL PLAYERS. Eh, George, George! Hast –
yaow! Look at him, fellas – he looks scared to death.
Yaow! George, don't look so innocent, you old
geezer. We know what you're thinking. Don't disgrace the team, big boy. Whoo-oo-oo.

STAGE MANAGER. All right! All right! That'll do. That's
enough of that.

(Smiling, he pushes them off the stage. They lean back
to shout a few more catcalls.)

There used to be an awful lot of that kind of thing at
weddings in the old days, – Rome, and later. We're
more civilized now, – so they say.

(The choir starts singing "Love Divine, All Love
Excelling –". George has reached the stage. He stares
at the congregation a moment, then takes a few steps of
withdrawal, toward the right proscenium pillar. His
mother, from the front row, seems to have felt his
confusion. She leaves her seat and comes down the
aisle quickly to him.)

MRS. GIBBS. George! George! What's the matter?

GEORGE. Ma, I don't want to grow old. Why's everybody pushing me so?

MRS. GIBBS. Why, George . . . you wanted it.

GEORGE. No, Ma, listen to me –

MRS. GIBBS. No, no, George, – you're a man now.

---

3 **to catcall:** zischen, buh rufen.
7 **geezer** (slang): Kerl, komischer Kauz.
7 f. **to disgrace:** Schande machen.
17 **to excel:** übertreffen.
19 **withdrawal:** Rückzug; Zurücktreten, Sich-Zurückziehen.

GEORGE. Listen, Ma, – for the last time I ask you . . . All
I want to do is to be a fella –

MRS. GIBBS. George! If anyone should hear you! Now
stop. Why, I'm ashamed of you!

5 GEORGE. (*He comes to himself and looks over the scene.*)
What? Where's Emily?

MRS. GIBBS (*relieved*). George! You gave me such a turn.

GEORGE. Cheer up, Ma. I'm getting married.

MRS. GIBBS. Let me catch my breath a minute.

10 GEORGE (*comforting her*). Now, Ma, you save Thursday
nights. Emily and I are coming over to dinner every
Thursday night . . . you'll see. Ma, what are you
crying for? Come on; we've got to get ready for this.
(*Mrs. Gibbs, mastering her emotion, fixes his tie and*
15 *whispers to him.*
In the meantime, Emily, in white and wearing her
wedding veil, has come through the audience and
mounted onto the stage. She too draws back, fright-
ened, when she sees the congregation in the church.
20 *The choir begins: "Blessed Be the Tie That Binds".*)

EMILY. I never felt so alone in my whole life. And
George over there, looking so . . .! I *hate* him. I wish I
were dead. Papa! Papa!

MR. WEBB (*leaves his seat in the pews and comes toward*
25 *her anxiously*). Emily! Emily! Now don't get upset. . . .

EMILY. But, Papa, – I don't want to get married. . . .

MR. WEBB. Sh – sh – Emily. Everything's all right.

EMILY. Why can't I stay for a while just as I am? Let's go
30 away, –

---

7 **to give s.o. a turn:** jdm. einen Schrecken einjagen.
25 f. **upset:** aufgeregt, durcheinander.

MR. WEBB. No, no, Emily. Now stop and think a minute.

EMILY. Don't you remember that you used to say, – all
the time you used to say – all the time: that I was *your*
girl! There must be lots of places we can go to. I'll
work for you. I could keep house.

MR. WEBB. Sh ... You mustn't think of such things.
You're just nervous, Emily.
(He turns and calls:)
George! George! Will you come here a minute?
(He leads her toward George.)
Why you're marrying the best young fellow in the
world. George is a fine fellow.

EMILY. But Papa, –
*(Mrs. Gibbs returns unobtrusively to her seat.
Mr. Webb has one arm around his daughter. He
places his hand on George's shoulder.)*

MR. WEBB. I'm giving away my daughter, George. Do
you think you can take care of her?

GEORGE. Mr. Webb, I want to ... I want to try. Emily,
I'm going to do my best. I love you, Emily. I need you.

EMILY. Well, if you love me, help me. All I want is
someone to love me.

GEORGE. I will, Emily. Emily, I'll try.

EMILY. And I mean for *ever*. Do you hear? For ever and
ever.
*(They fall into each other's arms.
The March from "Lohengrin" is heard.
The stage manager, as clergyman, stands on the box,
up center.)*

---

5 **to keep house:** den Haushalt führen.
17 **to give away** (*the bride*): (die Braut) übergeben (durch den Braut-
vater an den Bräutigam).
28 **clergyman:** Geistlicher.

MR. WEBB. Come, they're waiting for us. Now you know
it'll be all right. Come, quick.
*(George slips away and takes his place beside the stage
manager-clergyman.*

5   *Emily proceeds up the aisle on her father's arm.)*

STAGE MANAGER. Do you, George, take this woman,
Emily, to be your wedded wife, to have . . .
*(Mrs. Soames has been sitting in the last row of the
congregation.*

10   *She now turns to her neighbors and speaks in a shrill
voice. Her chatter drowns out the rest of the clergyman's words.)*

MRS. SOAMES. Perfectly lovely wedding! Loveliest wedding I ever saw. Oh, I do love a good wedding, don't

15   you? Doesn't she make a lovely bride?

GEORGE. I do.

STAGE MANAGER. Do you, Emily, take this man, George,
to be your wedded husband, –
(Again his further words are covered by those of Mrs.

20   *Soames.)*

MRS. SOAMES. Don't know *when* I've seen such a lovely
wedding. But I always cry. Don't know why it is, but I
always cry. I just like to see young people happy,
don't you? Oh, I think it's lovely.

25   *(The ring.*
The kiss.
The stage is suddenly arrested into silent tableau.
*The stage manager, his eyes on the distance, as though
to himself:)*

---

11 **to drown out:** hier: übertönen.
27 **silent tableau:** Tableau, zum Bild erstarrte Gruppierung auf der
Bühne.

STAGE MANAGER. I've married over two hundred couples in my day.

Do I believe in it?

I don't know.

5   M. . . . marries N. . . . millions of them.

The cottage, the go-cart, the Sunday-afternoon drives in the Ford, the first rheumatism, the grandchildren, the second rheumatism, the deathbed, the reading of the will, –

10   *(He now looks at the audience for the first time, with a warm smile that removes any sense of cynicism from the next line.)*

Once in a thousand times it's interesting.

– Well, let's have Mendelssohn's "Wedding March"!

15   *(The organ picks up the March.*

The bride and groom come down the aisle, radiant, but trying to be very dignified.)

MRS. SOAMES. Aren't they a lovely couple? Oh, I've never been to such a nice wedding. I'm sure they'll be

20   happy. I always say: *happiness*, that's the great thing! The important thing is to be happy.

(The bride and groom reach the steps leading into the audience. A bright light is thrown upon them. They descend into the auditorium and run up the aisle

25   *joyously.)*

STAGE MANAGER. That's all the Second Act folks. Ten minutes' intermission.

---

6 **go-cart:** Gängelwagen, Lauflernwagen ohne Boden.
11 **cynicism:** Zynismus.
15 **to pick up:** aufnehmen; hier: einsetzen mit.
16 **radiant:** strahlend.
17 **dignified:** würdevoll.
27 **intermission:** Pause, Unterbrechung.

Act III

During the intermission the audience has seen the stagehands arranging the stage. On the right-hand side, a little right of the center, ten or twelve ordinary chairs
5 *have been placed in three openly spaced rows facing the audience.*
These are graves in the cemetery.
Toward the end of the intermission the actors enter and take their places. The front row contains: toward the
10 *center of the stage, an empty chair; then Mrs. Gibbs; Simon Stimson.*
The second row contains, among others, Mrs. Soames.
The third row has Wally Webb.
The dead do not turn their heads or their eyes to right or
15 *left, but they sit in a quiet without stiffness. When they speak their tone is matter-of-fact, without sentimentality and, above all, without lugubriousness.*
The stage manager takes his accustomed place and waits for the house lights to go down.

20 STAGE MANAGER. This time nine years have gone by, friends – summer, 1913.

Gradual changes in Grover's Corners. Horses are getting rarer. Farmers coming into town in Fords.

---

5 **openly spaced:** mit Zwischenräumen.
16 **matter-of-fact:** sachlich, nüchtern.
  sentimentality: Sentimentalität, Rührseligkeit.
17 **lugubriousness:** Traurigkeit, Kummer.

Everybody locks their house doors now at night. Ain't been any burglars in town yet, but everybody's heard about 'em.

You'd be surprised, though – on the whole, things don't change much around here.

This is certainly an important part of Grover's Corners. It's on a hilltop – a windy hilltop – lots of sky, lots of clouds, – often lots of sun and moon and stars.

You come up here, on a fine afternoon and you can see range on range of hills – awful blue they are – up there by Lake Sunapee and Lake Winnipesaukee . . . and way up, if you've got a glass, you can see the White Mountains and Mt. Washington – where North Conway and Conway is. And, of course, our favorite mountain, Mt. Monadnock, 's right here – and all these towns that lie around it: Jaffrey, 'n East Jaffrey, 'n Peterborough, 'n Dublin; and *(then pointing down in the audience)* there, quite a ways down, is Grover's Corners.

Yes, beautiful spot up here. Mountain laurel and lilacks. I often wonder why people like to be buried in Woodlawn and Brooklyn when they might pass the same time up here in New Hampshire.

Over there – *(pointing to stage left)* are the old stones, – 1670, 1680. Strong-minded people that come a long way to be independent. Summer people walk around there laughing at the funny words on the tombstones . . .

---

2 **burglar:** Einbrecher.
21 **laurel:** Lorbeer.
21 f. **li-lack:** Flieder.
26 **strong-minded:** willensstark.

it don't do any harm. And genealogists come up from
Boston – get paid by city people for looking up their
ancestors. They want to make sure they're Daughters
of the American Revolution and of the *May-*
5 *flower*. . . . Well, I guess that don't do any harm,
either. Wherever you come near the human race,
there's layers and layers of nonsense. . . .
Over there are some Civil War veterans. Iron flags on
their graves . . . New Hampshire boys . . . had a
10 notion that the Union ought to be kept together,
though they'd never seen more than fifty miles of it
themselves. All they knew was the name, friends –
the United States of America. The United States of
America. And they went and died about it.
15 This here is the new part of the cemetery. Here's your
friend Mrs. Gibbs. 'N let me see – Here's Mr. Stimson, organist at the Congregational Church. And
Mrs. Soames who enjoyed the wedding so – you
remember? Oh, and a lot of others. And Editor
20 Webb's boy, Wallace, whose appendix burst while he
was on a Boy Scout trip to Crawford Notch.
Yes, an awful lot of sorrow has sort of quieted down
up here. People just wild with grief have brought
their relatives up to this hill. We all know how it is . . .
25 and then time . . . and sunny days . . . and rainy
days . . . 'n snow . . . We're all glad they're in a beauti-

---

1 **genealogist:** Genealoge, Familienforscher.
4 f. **Mayflower:** Name des Schiffs, mit dem 1620 die Quäker von England
    nach Amerika auswanderten.
7 **layer:** Schicht, Lage.
8 **veteran:** Veteran, ehemaliger Soldat.
20 **appendix:** Blinddarm.
21 **Boy Scout:** Pfadfinder.

ful place and we're coming up here ourselves when
our fit's over.

Now there are some things we all know, but we don't
take'm out and look at'm very often. We all know
that *something* is eternal. And it ain't houses and it
ain't names, and it ain't earth, and it ain't even the
stars ... everybody knows in their bones that *something* is eternal, and that something has to do with
human beings. All the greatest people ever lived have
been telling us that for five thousand years and yet
you'd be surprised how people are always losing hold
of it. There's something way down deep that's eternal
about every human being.

(Pause.)

You know as well as I do that the dead don't stay
interested in us living people for very long. Gradually, gradually, they lose hold of the earth ... and
the ambitions they had ... and the pleasures they
had ... and the things they suffered ... and the
people they loved.

They get weaned away from earth – that's the way I
put it, – weaned away.

And they stay here while the earth part of 'em burns
away, burns out; and all that time they slowly get indifferent to what's goin' on in Grover's Corners.

They're waitin'. They're waitin' for something that
they feel is comin'. Something important, and great.
Aren't they waitin' for the eternal part in them to
come out clear?

2 **fit:** Ausbruch, Anfall.
21 **to wean:** entwöhnen.

Some of the things they're going to say maybe'll hurt
your feelings – but that's the way it is: mother 'n
daughter ... husband 'n wife ... enemy 'n enemy ...
money 'n miser ... all those terribly important things
5 kind of grow pale around here. And what's left when
memory's gone, and your identity, Mrs. Smith?
*(He looks at the audience a minute, then turns to the
stage.)*
Well! There are some *living* people. There's Joe
10 Stoddard, our undertaker, supervising a new-made
grave. And here comes a Grover's Corners boy, that
left town to go out West.
*(Joe Stoddard has hovered about in the background.
Sam Craig enters left, wiping his forehead from the
15 exertion. He carries an umbrella and strolls front.)*

SAM CRAIG. Good afternoon, Joe Stoddard.

JOE STODDARD. Good afternoon, good afternoon. Let
me see now: do I know you?

SAM CRAIG. I'm Sam Craig.

20 JOE STODDARD. Gracious sakes' alive! Of all people! I
should'a knowed you'd be back for the funeral.
You've been away a long time, Sam.

SAM CRAIG. Yes, I've been away over twelve years. I'm
in business out in Buffalo now, Joe. But I was in the
25 East when I got news of my cousin's death, so I

---

4 **miser:** Geizhals.
6 **identity:** Identität.
10 **undertaker:** Leichenbestatter.
   to supervise: beaufsichtigen, überwachen.
13 **to hover:** schweben; hier: verweilen, sich (wartend) aufhalten.
15 **exertion:** Anstrengung.
20 **Of all people!:** Ausgerechnet du!

thought I'd combine things a little and come and see
the old home. You look well.

JOE STODDARD. Yes, yes, can't complain. Very sad, our
journey today, Samuel.

5 SAM CRAIG. Yes.

JOE STODDARD. Yes, yes. I always say I hate to supervise
when a young person is taken. They'll be here in a
few minutes now. I had to come here early today –
my son's supervisin' at the home.

10 SAM CRAIG (*reading stones*). Old Farmer McCarty, I
used to do chores for him – after school. He had the
lumbago.

JOE STODDARD. Yes, we brought Farmer McCarty here a
number of years ago now.

15 SAM CRAIG (*staring at Mrs. Gibbs' knees*). Why, this is
my Aunt Julia ... I'd forgotten that she'd ... of
course, of course.

JOE STODDARD. Yes, Doc Gibbs lost his wife two-three
years ago ... about this time. And today's another

20 pretty bad blow for him, too.

MRS. GIBBS (*to Simon Stimson: in an even voice*). That's
my sister Carey's boy, Sam ... Sam Craig.

SIMON STIMSON. I'm always uncomfortable when *they're*
around.

25 MRS. GIBBS. Simon.

SAM CRAIG. Do they choose their own verses much, Joe?

JOE STODDARD. No ... not usual. Mostly the bereaved
pick a verse.

---

11 **chores:** kleinere (Aushilfs-)Arbeiten (AE).
12 **lumbago:** Hexenschuß.
21 **even:** hier: gleichförmig.
27 **the bereaved:** die Hinterbliebenen.

SAM CRAIG. Doesn't sound like Aunt Julia. There aren't many of those Hersey sisters left now. Let me see: where are ... I wanted to look at my father's and mother's ...

5 JOE STODDARD. Over there with the Craigs ... Avenue F.

SAM CRAIG *(reading Simon Stimson's epitaph)*. He was organist at church, wasn't he? – Hm, drank a lot, we used to say.

10 JOE STODDARD. Nobody was supposed to know about it. He'd seen a peck of trouble.

(Behind his hand.)

Took his own life, y' know?

SAM CRAIG. Oh, did he?

15 JOE STODDARD. Hung himself in the attic. They tried to hush it up, but of course it got around. He chose his own epy-taph. You can see it there. It ain't a verse exactly.

SAM CRAIG. Why, it's just some notes of music – what 20 is it?

JOE STODDARD. Oh, I wouldn't know. It was wrote up in the Boston papers at the time.

SAM CRAIG. Joe, what did she die of?

JOE STODDARD. Who?

25 SAM CRAIG. My cousin.

JOE STODDARD. Oh, didn't you know? Had some trouble bringing a baby into the world. 'Twas her second, though. There's a little boy 'bout four years old.

---

7 **epitaph:** Grabinschrift.

15 **attic:** Dachboden.

16 **to hush s.th. up:** vertuschen, totschweigen.

SAM CRAIG *(opening his umbrella)*.
   The grave's going to be over there?

JOE STODDARD. Yes, there ain't much more room over
   here among the Gibbses, so they're opening up a
5 whole new Gibbs section over by Avenue B. You'll
   excuse me now. I see they're comin'.
   (From left to center, at the back of the stage, comes a
   procession. Four men carry a casket, invisible to us.
   All the rest are under umbrellas. One can vaguely see:
10 *Dr. Gibbs, George, the Webbs, etc. They gather about*
   a grave in the back center of the stage, a little to the left
   of center.)

MRS. SOAMES. Who is it, Julia?

MRS. GIBBS *(without raising her eyes)*. My daughter-in-
15 law, Emily Webb.

MRS. SOAMES *(a little surprised, but no emotion)*. Well, I
   declare! The road up here must have been awful
   muddy. What did she die of, Julia?

MRS. GIBBS. In childbirth.

20 MRS. SOAMES. Childbirth. *(Almost with a laugh.)* I'd
   forgotten all about that. My, wasn't life awful – *(with*
   a sigh) and wonderful.

SIMON STIMSON *(with a sideways glance)*. Wonderful,
   was it?

25 MRS. GIBBS. Simon! Now, remember!

MRS. SOAMES. I remember Emily's wedding. Wasn't it a
   lovely wedding! And I remember her reading the

---

8 **casket:** Sarg (AE).
9 **vaguely** (adv.): undeutlich, unklar.
18 **muddy:** schlammig, schmutzig.
19 **in childbirth:** im Kindbett.
23 **sideways glance:** Seitenblick.

class poem at Graduation Exercises. Emily was one
of the brightest girls ever graduated from High
School. I've heard Principal Wilkins say so time after
time. I called on them at their new farm, just before I
died. Perfectly beautiful farm.

A WOMAN FROM AMONG THE DEAD. It's on the same road
we lived on.

A MAN AMONG THE DEAD. Yepp, right smart farm.

(They subside. The group by the grave starts singing
"Blessed Be the Tie That Binds".)

A WOMAN AMONG THE DEAD. I always liked that hymn. I
was hopin' they'd sing a hymn.

(Pause. Suddenly Emily appears from among the
umbrellas. She is wearing a white dress. Her hair is
down her back and tied by a white ribbon like a little
girl. She comes slowly, gazing wonderingly at the
dead, a little dazed.

She stops halfway and smiles faintly. After looking at
the mourners for a moment, she walks slowly to the
vacant chair beside Mrs. Gibbs and sits down.)

EMILY *(to them all, quietly, smiling).* Hello.

MRS. SOAMES. Hello, Emily.

A MAN AMONG THE DEAD. Hello, M's Gibbs.

EMILY *(warmly).* Hello, Mother Gibbs.

MRS. GIBBS. Emily.

1 **Graduation Exercises:** Schulabschlußfeier.
3f. **time after time:** immer wieder.
8 **smart:** schmuck, hübsch.
9 **to subside:** hier: verstummen.
11 **hymn:** Kirchenlied, Choral.
17 **dazed:** verwirrt, benommen.
19 **mourner:** Trauernder.
20 **vacant:** leer, frei.

EMILY. Hello.
(With surprise.)
It's raining.
(Her eyes drift back to the funeral company.)

5 MRS. GIBBS. Yes . . . They'll be gone soon, dear. Just rest
yourself.

EMILY. It seems thousands and thousands of years since
I . . . Papa remembered that that was my favorite
hymn.

10 Oh, I wish I'd been here a long time. I don't like
being new here. – How do you do, Mr. Stimson?

SIMON STIMSON. How do you do, Emily.
*(Emily continues to look about her with a wondering
smile; as though to shut out from her mind the thought*

15 *of the funeral company she starts speaking to Mrs.
Gibbs with a touch of nervousness.)*

EMILY. Mother Gibbs, George and I have made that
farm into just the best place you ever saw. We
thought of you all the time. We wanted to show you

20 the new barn and a great long ce-ment drinking
fountain for the stock. We bought that out of the
money you left us.

MRS. GIBBS. I did?

EMILY. Don't you remember, Mother Gibbs – the legacy

25 you left us? Why, it was over three hundred and fifty
dollars.

MRS. GIBBS. Yes, yes, Emily.

EMILY. Well, there's a patent device on the drinking
fountain so that it never overflows, Mother Gibbs,

---

20 **ce-ment:** Zement.
20 f. **drinking fountain:** Trinkbrunnen.
28 **patent device:** Patentvorrichtung.

and it never sinks below a certain mark they have
there. It's fine.
*(Here voice trails off and her eyes return to the funeral
group.)*
5 It won't be the same to George without me, but it's a
lovely farm.
(Suddenly she looks directly at Mrs. Gibbs.)
Live people don't understand, do they?

MRS. GIBBS. No, dear – not very much.

10 EMILY. They're sort of shut up in little boxes, aren't
they? I feel as though I knew them last a thousand
years ago ... My boy is spending the day at Mrs.
Carter's.
(She sees Mr. Carter among the dead.)
15 Oh, Mr. Carter, my little boy is spending the day at
your house.

MR. CARTER. Is he?

EMILY. Yes, he loves it there. – Mother Gibbs, we have a
Ford, too. Never gives any trouble. I don't drive,
20 though. Mother Gibbs, when does this feeling go
away? – Of being ... one of *them*? How long does
it ...?

MRS. GIBBS. Sh! dear. Just wait and be patient.

EMILY *(with a sigh)*. I know. – Look, they're finished.
25 They're going.

MRS. GIBBS. Sh –.
*(The umbrellas leave the stage. Dr. Gibbs has come
over to his wife's grave and stands before it a moment.
Emily looks up at his face. Mrs. Gibbs does not raise
30 her eyes.)*

---

3 **to trail off:** leiser, schwächer werden.
8 **live:** lebendig.

EMILY. Look! Father Gibbs is bringing some of my
flowers to you. He looks just like George, doesn't
he? Oh, Mother Gibbs, I never realized before how
troubled and how ... how in the dark live persons
5   are. Look at him. I loved him so. From morning till
night, that's all they are – troubled.
(Dr. Gibbs goes off.)

THE DEAD. Little cooler than it was. – Yes, that rain's
cooled it off a little. Those northeast winds always do
10   the same thing, don't they? If it isn't a rain, it's a
three-day blow. –
*(A patient calm falls on the stage. The stage manager
appears at his proscenium pillar, smoking. Emily sits
up abruptly with an idea.)*

15 EMILY. But, Mother Gibbs, one can go back; one can go
back there again ... into living. I feel it. I know it.
Why just then for a moment I was thinking about ...
about the farm ... and for a minute I *was* there, and
my baby was on my lap as plain as day.

20 MRS. GIBBS. Yes, of course you can.

EMILY. I can go back there and live all those days over
again ... why not?

MRS. GIBBS. All I can say is, Emily, don't.

EMILY. *(She appeals urgently to the stage manger.)* But
25   it's true, isn't it? I can go and live ... back there ...
again.

STAGE MANAGER. Yes, some have tried – but they soon
come back here.

MRS. GIBBS. Don't do it, Emily.

---

11 **blow:** hier: Sturm.
19 **as plain as day:** ganz offensichtlich.
24 **urgently** (adv.): dringend, drängend.

MRS. SOAMES. Emily, don't. It's not what you think
it'd be.

EMILY. But I won't live over a sad day. I'll choose a
happy one – I'll choose the day I first knew that I
5   loved George. Why should that be painful?
*(They are silent. Her question turns to the stage man-
ager.)*

STAGE MANAGER. You not only live it; but you watch
yourself living it.

10 EMILY. Yes?

STAGE MANAGER. And as you watch it, you see the thing
that they – down there – never know. You see the
future. You know what's going to happen afterwards.

EMILY. But is that – painful? Why?

15 MRS. GIBBS. That's not the only reason why you shouldn't
do it, Emily. When you've been here longer you'll see
that our life here is to forget all that, and think only of
what's ahead, and be ready for what's ahead. When
you've been here longer you'll understand.

20 EMILY *(softly)*. But, Mother Gibbs, how can I *ever*
forget that life? It's all I know. It's all I had.

MRS. SOAMES. Oh, Emily. It isn't wise. Really, it isn't.

EMILY. But it's a thing I must know by myself. I'll choose
a happy day, anyway.

25 MRS. GIBBS. *No!* – At least, choose an unimportant day.
Choose the least important day in your life. It will be
important enough.

EMILY *(to herself)*. Then it can't be since I was married;
or since the baby was born.

30 *(To the stage manager, eagerly.)*

---

24 **anyway:** jedenfalls, sowieso, ohnehin.

I can choose a birthday at least, can't I? – I choose my
twelfth birthday.

STAGE MANAGER. All right. February 11th, 1899. A
Tuesday. – Do you want any special time of day?

5 EMILY. Oh, I want the whole day.

STAGE MANAGER. We'll begin at dawn. You remember it
had been snowing for several days; but it had stopped
the night before, and they had begun clearing the
roads. The sun's coming up.

10 EMILY *(with a cry; rising)*. There's Main Street . . . why,
that's Mr. Morgan's drugstore before he changed
it! . . . And there's the livery stable.
*(The stage at no time in this act has been very dark; but
now the left half of the stage gradually becomes very*
15 *bright – the brightness of a crisp winter morning.
Emily walks toward Main Street.)*

STAGE MANAGER. Yes, it's 1899. This is fourteen years
ago.

EMILY. Oh, that's the town I knew as a little girl. And,
20 *look*, there's the old white fence that used to be
around our house. Oh, I'd forgotten that! Oh, I love
it so! Are they inside?

STAGE MANAGER. Yes, your mother'll be coming downstairs in a minute to make breakfast.

25 EMILY *(softly)*. Will she?

STAGE MANAGER. And you remember: your father had
been away for several days; he came back on the
early-morning train.

EMILY. No . . . ?

12 **livery stable:** Mietstall.
15 **crisp:** frisch, kalt und klar.

STAGE MANAGER. He'd been back to his college to make
a speech – in western New York, at Clinton.

EMILY. Look! There's Howie Newsome. There's our
policeman. But he's *dead*; he died.

5 *(The voices of Howie Newsome, Constable Warren*
and Joe Crowell, Jr., are heard at the left of the stage.
Emily listens in delight.)

HOWIE NEWSOME. Whoa, Bessie! – Bessie! 'Morning,
Bill.

10 CONSTABLE WARREN. Morning, Howie.

HOWIE NEWSOME. You're up early.

CONSTABLE WARREN. Been rescuin' a party; darn near
froze to death, down by Polish Town thar. Got drunk
and lay out in the snowdrifts. Thought he was in bed

15 when I shook'm.

EMILY. Why, there's Joe Crowell. . . .

JOE CROWELL. Good morning, Mr. Warren. 'Morning,
Howie.

(Mrs. Webb has appeared in her kitchen, but Emily

20 *does not see her until she calls.)*

MRS. WEBB. Chil-*dren!* Wally! Emily! . . . Time to get up.

EMILY. Mama, I'm here! Oh! how young Mama looks! I
didn't know Mama was ever that young.

MRS. WEBB. You can come and dress by the kitchen fire,

25 if you like; but hurry.

(Howie Newsome has entered along Main Street and
brings the milk to Mrs. Webb's door.)

Good morning, Mr. Newsome. Whhhh – it's cold.

HOWIE NEWSOME. Ten below by my barn, Mrs. Webb.

---

12 **party:** hier: Kerl, Mensch.
13 **thar:** *there.*
14 **snowdrift:** Schneewehe.

MRS. WEBB. Think of it! Keep yourself wrapped up.
(She takes her bottles in, shuddering.)

EMILY *(with an effort)*. Mama, I can't find my blue hair
ribbon anywhere.

5 MRS. WEBB. Just open your eyes, dear, that's all. I laid it
out for you special – on the dresser, there. If it were a
snake it would bite you.

EMILY. Yes, yes ...
(She puts her hand on her heart. Mr. Webb comes
10 *along Main Street, where he meets Constable Warren.*
Their movements and voices are increasingly lively in
the sharp air.)

MR. WEBB. Good morning, Bill.

CONSTABLE WARREN. Good morning, Mr. Webb. You're
15 up early.

MR. WEBB. Yes, just been back to my old college in New
York State. Been any trouble here?

CONSTABLE WARREN. Well, I was called up this mornin'
to rescue a Polish fella – darn near froze to death he
20 was.

MR. WEBB. We must get it in the paper.

CONSTABLE WARREN. 'Twan't much.

EMILY *(whispers)*. Papa.
(Mr. Webb shakes the snow off his feet and enters his
25 *house. Constable Warren goes off, right.)*

MR. WEBB. Good morning, Mother.

MRS. WEBB. How did it go, Charles?

MR. WEBB. Oh, fine, I guess. I told'm a few things. –
Everything all right here?

---

1 **Think of it!:** Denk mal an!
2 **to shudder:** schaudern.
5f. **to lay out:** zurecht-, herauslegen.
6 **dresser:** Anrichte.

MRS. WEBB. Yes – can't think of anything that's happened, special. Been right cold. Howie Newsome says it's ten below over to his barn.

MR. WEBB. Yes, well, it's colder than that at Hamilton
5   College. Students' ears are falling off. It ain't Christian. – Paper have any mistakes in it?

MRS. WEBB. None that I noticed. Coffee's ready when you want it.

(He starts upstairs.)

10   Charles! Don't forget; it's Emily's birthday. Did you remember to get her something?

MR. WEBB *(patting his pocket).* Yes, I've got something here.

(Calling up the stairs.)

15   Where's my girl? Where's my birthday girl?

(He goes off left.)

MRS. WEBB. Don't interrupt her now, Charles. You can see her at breakfast. She's slow enough as it is. Hurry up, children! It's seven o'clock. Now, I don't want to
20   call you again.

EMILY *(softly, more in wonder than in grief).* I can't bear it. They're so young and beautiful. Why did they ever have to get old? Mama, I'm here. I'm grown up. I love you all, everything. – I can't look at everything
25   hard enough.

(She looks questioningly at the stage manager, saying or suggesting: "Can I go in?" He nods briefly. She crosses to the inner door to the kitchen, left of her

---

12 **to pat:** (be)klopfen.
26 **questioningly** (adv.): fragend.
27 **to suggest:** andeuten.

mother, and as though entering the room, says, suggesting the voice of a girl of twelve:)
Good morning, Mama.

MRS. WEBB *(crossing to embrace and kiss her; in her*
5 *characteristic matter-of-fact manner).* Well, now,
dear, a very happy birthday to my girl and many
happy returns. There are some surprises waiting for
you on the kitchen table.

EMILY. Oh, Mama, you *shouldn't* have.
10 *(She throws an anguished glance at the stage manager.)*
I can't – I can't.

MRS. WEBB *(facing the audience, over her stove).* But
birthday or no birthday, I want you to eat your
15 breakfast good and slow. I want you to grow up and
be a good strong girl.
That in the blue paper is from your Aunt Carrie; and
I reckon you can guess who brought the post-card
album. I found it on the doorstep when I brought in
20 the milk – George Gibbs . . . must have come over in
the cold pretty early . . . right nice of him.

EMILY *(to herself).* Oh, George! I'd forgotten that. . . .

MRS. WEBB. Chew that bacon good and slow. It'll help
keep you warm on a cold day.

25 EMILY *(with mounting urgency).* Oh, Mama, just look at
me one minute as though you really saw me. Mama,
fourteen years have gone by. I'm dead. You're a
grandmother, Mama. I married George Gibbs, Mama.

---

10 **anguished:** gepeinigt.
23 **to chew:** kauen.
25 **urgency:** Dringlichkeit.

Wally's dead, too. Mama, his appendix burst on a camping trip to North Conway. We felt just terrible about it – don't you remember? But, just for a moment now we're all together. Mama, just for a
5 moment we're happy. *Let's look at one another.*

MRS. WEBB. That in the yellow paper is something I found in the attic among your grandmother's things. You're old enough to wear it now, and I thought you'd like it.

10 EMILY. And this is from you. Why, Mama, it's just lovely and it's just what I wanted. It's beautiful!
(She flings her arms around her mother's neck. Her mother goes on with her cooking, but is pleased.)

MRS. WEBB. Well, I hoped you'd like it. Hunted all over.
15 Your Aunt Norah couldn't find one in Concord, so I had to send all the way to Boston.
(Laughing.)
Wally has something for you, too. He made it at manual-training class and he's very proud of it. Be
20 sure you make a big fuss about it. – Your father has a surprise for you, too; don't know what it is myself. Sh – here he comes.

MR. WEBB *(off stage).* Where's my girl? Where's my birthday girl?

25 EMILY *(in a loud voice to the stage manager).* I can't. I can't go on. It goes so fast. We don't have time to look at one another.
(She breaks down sobbing.
The lights dim on the left half of the stage. Mrs. Webb
30 *disappears.)*

---

19 **manual-training class:** Werkunterricht.
20 **a big fuss:** viel Aufhebens.

I didn't realize. So all that was going on and we never
noticed. Take me back – up the hill – to my grave.
But first: Wait! One more look.
Good-by, Good-by, world. Good-by, Grover's Cor-
5 ners ... Mama and Papa. Good-by to clocks tick-
ing ... and Mama's sunflowers. And food and coffee.
And new-ironed dresses and hot baths ... and sleep-
ing and waking up. Oh, earth, you're too wonderful
for anybody to realize you.
10 *(She looks toward the stage manager and asks
abruptly, through her tears:)*
Do any human beings ever realize life while they live
it? – every, every minute?
STAGE MANAGER. No.
15 *(Pause.)*
The saints and poets, maybe – they do some.
EMILY. I'm ready to go back.
*(She returns to her chair beside Mrs. Gibbs.
Pause.)*
20 MRS. GIBBS. Were you happy?
EMILY. No ... I should have listened to you. That's all
human beings are! Just blind people.
MRS. GIBBS. Look, it's clearing up. The stars are coming
out.
25 EMILY. Oh, Mr. Stimson, I should have listened to them.
SIMON STIMSON *(with mounting violence; bitingly.)* Yes,
now you know. Now you know! That's what it was to
be alive. To move about in a cloud of ignorance; to go
up and down trampling on the feelings of those ... of
30 those about you. To spend and waste time as though

---

29 **to trample:** trampeln, treten.

you had a million years. To be always at the mercy
of one self-centered passion, or another. Now you
know – that's the happy existence you wanted to go
back to. Ignorance and blindness.

5 MRS. GIBBS (*spiritedly*). Simon Stimson, that ain't the
whole truth and you know it. Emily, look at that star.
I forget its name.

A MAN AMONG THE DEAD. My boy Joel was a sailor, –
knew 'em all. He'd set on he porch evenings and tell
10 'em all by name. Yes, sir, wonderful!

ANOTHER MAN AMONG THE DEAD. <u>A star's mighty good
company.</u>

A WOMAN AMONG THE DEAD. Yes. Yes, 'tis.

SIMON STIMSON. Here's one of *them* coming.

15 THE DEAD. That's funny. 'Tain't no time for one of them
to be here. – Goodness sakes.

EMILY. Mother Gibbs, it's George.

MRS. GIBBS. Sh, dear. Just rest yourself.

EMILY. It's George.

20 (*George enters from the left, and slowly comes toward
them.*)

A MAN FROM AMONG THE DEAD. And my boy, Joel, who
knew the stars – he used to say it took millions of
years for that speck o' light to git to the earth. Don't
25 seem like a body could believe it, but that's what he
used to say – millions of years.

(*George sinks to his knees then falls full length at
Emily's feet.*)

---

1 f. **to be at the mercy of:** ausgeliefert, preisgegeben sein.
2 **self-centered:** egozentrisch, ichbezogen.
5 **spiritedly** (adv.): lebhaft, energisch.
9 **porch:** Veranda (vor dem Haus).
24 **speck:** Fleck.
27 **full length:** der Länge nach.

A WOMAN AMONG THE DEAD. Goodness! That ain't no
way to behave!

MRS. SOAMES. He ought to be home.

EMILY. Mother Gibbs?

5 MRS. GIBBS. Yes, Emily?

EMILY. They don't understand, do they?

MRS. GIBBS. No, dear. They don't understand.

(The stage manager appears at the right, one hand on a
dark curtain which he slowly draws across the
10 *scene.*

In the distance a clock is heard striking the hour very
faintly.)

STAGE MANAGER. Most everybody's asleep in Grover's
Corners. There are a few lights on: Shorty Hawkins,
15 down at the depot, has just watched the Albany train
go by. And at the livery stable somebody's setting up
late and talking. – Yes, it's clearing up. There are the
stars – doing their old, old crisscross journeys in the
sky. Scholars haven't settled the matter yet, but they
20 seem to think there are no living beings up there. Just
chalk ... or fire. Only this one is straining away,
straining away all the time to make something of
itself. The strain's so bad that every sixteen hours
everybody lies down and gets a rest.

25 *(He winds his watch.)*

Hm. ... Eleven o'clock in Grover's Corners. – You
get a good rest, too. Good night.

---

18 **crisscross:** sich kreuzend, kreuz und quer.
19 **to settle:** hier: entscheiden.
21 **to strain:** sich mühen, anstrengen.
   away: hier: immerzu, drauflos.
23 **strain:** Anstrengung, Anspannung.

Editorische Notiz

Der englische Text folgt der Ausgabe: *Three Plays (Our Town, The Skin of Our Teeth, The Matchmaker)* by Thornton Wilder, New York: Harper & Brothers, o. J. Das Glossar erklärt in der Regel alle Wörter, die über die Wertigkeitsstufe 4 des *Englischen Arbeitswörterbuches* von Alfred Haase (Frankfurt a. M.: Moritz Diesterweg, [7]1979) hinausgehen. Im Zweifelsfall wurde großzügig verfahren, d. h. eher eine Vokabel mehr aufgenommen als dort vorgesehen.

Im Glossar verwendete Abkürzungen

adv.	adverb
AE	American English
arch.	archaic (veraltet)
coll.	colloquial (umgangssprachlich)
frz.	französisch
o.s.	oneself
pl.	plural
poet.	poetical (dichterisch, gehoben)
s.o.	someone
s.th.	something

Literaturhinweise

I. *Werke*

a) Dramen

The Angel that Troubled the Waters and Other Plays, New York: Coward-McCann, 1928.

The Long Christmas Dinner & Other Plays in One Act, New York: Coward-McCann / New Haven, Conn.: Yale University Press, 1931.

Out Town. A Play in Three Acts, New York: Coward-McCann, 1938.

The Merchant of Yonkers. A Farce in Four Acts, New York: Harper, 1939.

The Skin of Our Teeth. A Play in Three Acts, New York: Harper, 1942.

Three Plays: Our Town / The Skin of Our Teeth / The Matchmaker, New York: Harper, 1957. [Diese Ausgabe enthält die revidierte Fassung von *Our Town*.]

The Alcestiad or A Life in the Sun. A Play in Three Acts with a Satyr Play, The Drunken Sisters, New York: Harper and Row, 1977.

b) Romane

The Cabala, New York: Albert and Charles Boni, 1926.

The Bridge of San Luis Rey, New York: Albert and Charles Boni, 1927.

The Woman of Andros, New York: Albert and Charles Boni, 1930.

Heaven's My Destination, New York: Harper, 1935.

The Ides of March, New York: Harper, 1948.

The Eighth Day, New York: Harper and Row, 1967.

Theophilus North, New York: Harper and Row, 1973.

c) Theoretische Äußerungen

»Some Thoughts on Playwriting«, in: *The Intent of the Artist*,
ed. by Augusto Centeno, Princeton, N. J., 1941, S. 83–98;
auch in: *Playwrights on Playwriting*, ed. by Toby Cole, New
York 1960, S. 106–115; dt.: »Einige Gedanken über das
Schreiben von Theaterstücken«, übers. von Herberth E.
Herlitschka, in: *Amerikanische Dramaturgie*, hrsg. von
Horst Frenz unter Mitarbeit von Claus Clüver, Reinbek bei
Hamburg 1962, S. 18–27.

»Kultur in einer Demokratie«, in: *Drei Ansprachen anläßlich
der Verleihung des Friedenspreises des Deutschen Buchhan-
dels*, Frankfurt a. M. 1957.

»Thornton Wilder«, in: *Writers at Work. The Paris Review
Interviews*, ed. by Malcolm Cowley, New York 1958,
S. 101–118. [Interview von Richard H. Goldstone mit
Thornton Wilder.]

d) Übersetzung von *Our Town*

Unsere kleine Stadt. Schauspiel in drei Akten, ins Deutsche
übertragen von Hans Sahl, Frankfurt a. M. 1957 (S. Fischer
Schulausgaben moderner Autoren).

II. *Bibliographien*

Edelstein, J. M., comp., *A Bibliographical Checklist of the
Writings of Thornton Wilder*, New Haven, Conn.: Yale
University Library, 1959.

Goldstone, Richard H. / Anderson, Gary, *Thornton Wilder.
An Annotated Bibliography of Works by and about Thornton Wilder*, New York 1982.

Kosok, Heinz, »Thornton Wilder. A Bibliography of Criti-
cism«, in: *Twentieth Century Literature* 9 (1963) S. 93–100.

– »Thornton Wilder. Ein Literaturbericht«, in: *Jahrbuch für
Amerikastudien* 9 (1964) S. 196–227.

III. *Sekundärliteratur*

Atkinson, Brooks, »Mrs. Roosevelt on *Our Town*«, in: G. Oppenheimer (Hrsg.), *The Passionate Playgoer*, New York 1958, S. 541–544.

Ballet, Arthur H., »In Our Living and in Our Dying«, in: *English Journal* 45 (1956) S. 243–249.

Beckmann, Heinz, *Thornton Wilder,* Hannover 1966 (Friedrichs Dramatiker des Welttheaters, Bd. 16).

Brown, John Mason, *Two on the Aisle*, New York 1938.

Burbank, Rex, *Thornton Wilder*, New York 1961, ²1978.

Burckhardt, Carl J., *Thornton Wilder. Ansprache bei der Verleihung des Friedenspreises an Thornton Wilder*, in: C. J. B., *Bildnisse*, Frankfurt a. M. 1958, S. 282–296.

Clüver, Claus, *Thornton Wilder und André Obey. Untersuchungen zum modernen epischen Theater*, Bonn 1978.

Cowley, Malcolm, »The Man Who Abolished Time«, in: *Saturday Review* 39 (6. Okt. 1956) S. 13 f., 50–52.

D'Ambrosio, Michael A., »Is ›Our Town‹ Really Our Town?«, in: *English Record* 22 (1971) S. 20–22.

Fergusson, Francis, »Three Allegorists: Brecht, Wilder and Eliot«, in: *Sewanee Review* 64 (1956) S. 544–573.

Frenz, Horst, »The Reception of Thornton Wilder's Plays in Germany«, in: *Modern Drama* 3 (1960) S. 123–137.

Frey, John R., »Postwar German Reactions to American Literature«, in: *Journal of English and German Philology* 54 (1955) S. 173–194.

Fulton, A. R., »Expressionism – Twenty Years After«, in: *Sewanee Review* 52 (1944) S. 398–413.

Gold, Michael, »Thornton Wilder: Prophet of the Genteel Christ«, in: *New Republic* 64 (22. Okt. 1930) S. 266 f.

Goldstein, Malcolm, *The Art of Thornton Wilder*, Lincoln, Neb., 1965.

Goldstone, Richard H., *Thornton Wilder: An Intimate Portrait*, New York 1975.

Grebanier, Bernard, *Thornton Wilder*, Minneapolis 1964.

Grenzmann, Wilhelm, »Thornton Wilder«, in: W. G., *Welt-*

dichtung der Gegenwart: Probleme und Gestalten, Bonn 1955, S. 426–446.

Haas, Rudolf, »Thornton Wilders *Our Town*: Gedanken zur wissenschaftlichen und unterrichtlichen Erschließung eines modernen amerikanischen Dramas«, in: *Mitteilungsblatt des Allgemeinen Deutschen Neuphilologenverbandes* 14 (1961) S. 42–46; auch in: Hans Itschert (Hrsg.), *Das amerikanische Drama von den Anfängen bis zur Gegenwart*, Darmstadt 1972, S. 209–217.

Haberman, Donald, *The Plays of Thornton Wilder*, Middletown, Conn., 1967.

Häberle, Erwin, *Das szenische Werk Thornton Wilders*, Heidelberg 1967 (Jahrbuch für Amerikastudien, Beih. 24).

Herms, Dieter, »Zum Humor im epischen Theater Thornton Wilders«, in: *Die Neueren Sprachen* 20 (1971) S. 36–47.

Jäger, Dietrich, »Über Episches und Dramatisches im neueren Drama«, in: *Literatur in Wissenschaft und Unterricht* 11 (1978) S. 75–95.

Kesting, Marianne, *Das epische Theater: Zur Struktur des modernen Dramas*, Stuttgart [7]1978.

Klotz, Volker, »Thornton Wilders *Unsere kleine Stadt*«, in: *Das neue Forum* 9 (1959/60) S. 56–64.

Kuner, Mildred C., *Thornton Wilder: The Bright and the Dark*, New York 1972.

Link, Franz H., »Das Theater Thornton Wilders«, in: *Die Neueren Sprachen* 14 (1965) S. 305–318; auch in: Hans Itschert (Hrsg.), *Das amerikanische Drama von den Anfängen bis zur Gegenwart*, Darmstadt 1972, S. 177–194.

McCarthy, Mary, *Sights and Spectacles 1937–1956*, New York 1956.

Mennemeier, Franz Norbert, »Thornton Wilder«, in: F. N. M., *Das moderne Drama des Auslands*, Düsseldorf 1976, S. 94–109.

Papajewski, Helmut, *Thornton Wilder*, Frankfurt/Bonn 1961.

Porter, Thomas E., »A Green Corner of the Universe: *Our Town*«, in: T. E. P., *Myth and Modern American Drama*, Detroit 1969, S. 200–224.

Sahl, Hans, »Thornton Wilder: Skizzen zu einem Portrait«, in: *Perspektiven* 8 (1954) S. 64–82.

Schik, Berthold, »Problematisierung des Banalen – Thornton Wilders *Our Town* als Standardlektüre im Englischunterricht der Oberstufe?«, in: *Die Neueren Sprachen* 24 (1975) S. 429–443.

Schimpf, Sigurd, *Thornton Wilders Theaterstücke und ihre Inszenierungen auf den deutschen Bühnen*, Diss. Köln 1964.

Schöpp, Joseph C., »Thornton Wilders *Our Town*: theoretischer Anspruch und künstlerische Realisierung«, in: Alfred Weber / Siegfried Neuweiler (Hrsg.), *Amerikanisches Drama und Theater im 20. Jahrhundert*, Göttingen 1975, S. 148–170.

Scott, Winfield T., »*Our Town* and the Golden Veil«, in: *Virginia Quarterly Review* 29 (1953) S. 103–117.

Sell, Rainer, *Darstellung und Funktion des Todes im Werk Thornton Wilders unter besonderer Berücksichtigung von ›Our Town‹*, Diss. Kiel 1969.

Stephens, George D., »*Our Town* – Great American Tragedy?«, in: *Modern Drama* 1 (1959) S. 258–264.

Stresau, Hermann, *Thornton Wilder*, Berlin 1963.

Stürzl, Erwin, »Weltbild und Lebensphilosophie Thornton Wilders«, in: *Die Neueren Sprachen* 4 (1955), S. 341–351.

Szondi, Peter, *Theorie des modernen Dramas*, Frankfurt 1956.

Viebrock, Helmut, »Thornton Wilders Hauptmotiv«, in: *Die Neueren Sprachen* 10 (1961) S. 349–363.

Weber, Alfred, »*Our Town*« in: Werner Hüllen / Wilhelm Rossi / Walter Christopeit (Hrsg.), *Zeitgenössische amerikanische Dichter: Eine Einführung in die amerikanische Literaturbetrachtung*, Frankfurt a. M. 1960, S. 180–185.

Wells, Arvin R. / Hagopian, John V., »*Our Town*«, in: J. V. H. / M. Dolch (Hrsg.), *Insight I: Analyses of American Literature*, Frankfurt a. M. 1962, S. 264–271.

Wixson, Douglas C., jr., »The Dramatic Techniques of Thornton Wilder and Bertolt Brecht: A Study in Comparison«, in: *Modern Drama* 15 (1972) S. 112–124.

Zeittafel

17. 4. 1897	Geburt von Thornton Niven Wilder in Madison, Wisconsin, als Sohn des Politikwissenschaftlers und Journalisten Amos Parker Wilder und der Pfarrerstochter Isabella Thornton Niven Wilder.
1906	sechsmonatiger Aufenthalt in Hongkong aufgrund der Tätigkeit seines Vaters als Generalkonsul; Besuch der dortigen deutschen Schule.
1906–09	Aufenthalt in Berkeley, Kalifornien; Besuch der dortigen Schule.
1909	Aufenthalt in Shanghai; Besuch der deutschen Schule sowie einer chinesischen Missionsschule.
1910–15	Besuch eines Internates in Ojai, Kalifornien, sowie der Berkeley High School; erste kurze Theaterszenen.
1915–17	Besuch des Oberlin College, Ohio; Veröffentlichung einiger Einakter im *Oberlin Literary Magazin*.
1917–18	Besuch der Yale University.
1918–19	Teilnahme am Ersten Weltkrieg als Korporal der First Coast Artillery.
1919	Rückkehr zur Yale University.
1920–21	Studienjahr an der American Academy in Rom: Kurse in Archäologie, Beschäftigung mit klassischen Sprachen und Literatur.
1921–25	Tätigkeit als Französischlehrer an der Lawrenceville School in Princeton, New Jersey.
1924	Stipendium für die MacDowell Colony in Peterborough, New Hampshire; Rezensionen für *Theatre Arts Monthly*.
1926	Veröffentlichung des ersten Romans, *The Cabala*; erste professionelle Aufführung des frühen Stückes *The Trumpet Shall Sound*; Europareise, Begegnung mit Ernest Hemingway.
1927	Veröffentlichung von *The Bridge of San Luis Rey*;

	Fortsetzung der Tätigkeit an der Lawrenceville School.
1928	Pulitzer-Preis; Europareise; Veröffentlichung von *The Angel that Troubled the Waters and Other Plays*, einer Sammlung von sechzehn ›Dreiminutenspielen‹.
1929	Vortragsreisen und Beginn der Lehrtätigkeit an der Universität von Chicago.
1930	Veröffentlichung von *The Woman of Andros*.
1931	Veröffentlichung von *The Long Christmas Dinner and Other Plays in One Act*.
1932	Übersetzung und Bearbeitung von André Obeys *Le Viol de Lucrèce*.
1934	Veröffentlichung von *Heaven's My Destination*.
1935	Beginn der Freundschaft mit Gertrude Stein.
1937	Übersetzung von Ibsens *Nora*.
1938	Veröffentlichung von *Our Town*; Pulitzer-Preis; Veröffentlichung von *The Merchant of Yonkers* (basierend auf Nestroys *Einen Jux will er sich machen*, 1955 überarbeitet als *The Matchmaker*).
1940	Drehbuch zur Verfilmung von *Our Town*.
1942	Veröffentlichung von *The Skin of Our Teeth*; Pulitzer-Preis; Filmskript *The Shadow of a Doubt* für Alfred Hitchcock.
1942–45	Teilnahme am Zweiten Weltkrieg in Afrika und Italien.
1948	Veröffentlichung von *The Ides of March*.
1950–51	Charles-Eliot-Norton-Professur an der Harvard University.
1952	Auszeichnung mit der Goldmedaille der American Academy of Arts and Letters.
1955	Aufführung von *The Alcestiad* beim Festival von Edinburgh unter dem Titel *A Life in the Sun* (Veröffentlichung in Amerika erst 1977).
1957	Auszeichnung mit dem Friedenspreis des Deutschen Buchhandels.

1961	Uraufführung der Oper *Das lange Weihnachtsmahl* von Paul Hindemith.
1962	Aufführungen von Stücken aus den unvollendeten Zyklen *The Seven Deadly Sins* und *The Seven Ages of Man*; Uraufführung der Oper *The Alcestiad* von Louise Talma.
1963	Auszeichnung mit der Presidential Medal of Freedom.
1965	Auszeichnung mit der National Medal of Literature.
1967	Veröffentlichung von *The Eighth Day*; National Book Award.
1973	Veröffentlichung von *Theophilus North*.
7. 12. 1975	Tod Thornton Wilders in Hamden, Connecticut.
1997	Feiern zum 100. Geburtstag von Thornton Wilder in vielen Ländern.

Nachwort

Thornton Wilders Drama *Our Town* (1938) hat in der Kritik
von Anfang an ein sehr unterschiedliches Echo gefunden, und
daran hat sich bis heute grundsätzlich nichts geändert, wenn
auch die Positionen der Kritik durch die seither vergangene
Zeit sowie durch eine veränderte Forschungslage modifiziert
wurden. Das Stück, das 1938 den Pulitzer-Preis erhielt und
einen Kritiker zu dem Urteil veranlaßte, es sei *das* große
amerikanische Drama,[1] das im Nachkriegsdeutschland Begei-
sterung auslöste[2] und das dem Drama schlechthin neue Wege
zu weisen schien, wurde jedoch auch, sowohl aufgrund seiner
Thematik als auch seiner Form, aufs schärfste kritisiert und als
verlogen, pseudohumanistisch und als formalistische Spielerei
abgewertet.[3] Die Feststellung, das Stück wie das Gesamtwerk
Wilders seien von der Forschung längst noch nicht gebührend
und philologisch erschöpfend berücksichtigt,[4] ging einher mit
seiner zunehmenden Verdrängung von amerikanischen wie
auch deutschen Bühnen.[5] *Our Town* erwarb sich den fragwürdigen Ruf eines Klassikers für den Schulunterricht,[6] doch auch
dieser blieb nicht unangetastet, sowohl weil es als zu schwierig,[7]

---

1 Vgl. Arthur Ballet, »In Our Living and in Our Dying«, in: *English Journal*
   45 (1956) S. 243–249.
2 Mit der Rezeption in Deutschland beschäftigt sich vor allem Sigurd Schimpf,
   *Thornton Wilders Theaterstücke und ihre Inszenierungen auf den deutschen
   Bühnen*, Diss. Köln 1964.
3 Vgl. Eberhard Brüning, *Das amerikanische Drama der dreißiger Jahre*, Berlin
   1966, S. 69 f.
4 Vgl. Claus Clüver, *Thornton Wilder und André Obey. Untersuchungen zum
   modernen epischen Theater*, Bonn 1978, S. X.
5 Vgl. das Urteil von Berthold Schik: »eine Erkenntnis [. . .], die bei den
   Dramaturgen deutscher Theater bereits zum Allgemeingut geworden ist: die
   Erkenntnis nämlich, daß *Our Town* sich heute kaum noch aufführen läßt.«
   B. Sch., »Problematisierung des Banalen – Thornton Wilders *Our Town* als
   Standardlektüre im Englischunterricht der Oberstufe?«, in: *Die Neueren
   Sprachen* 24 (1975) S. 441.
6 Hinweise für die unterrichtliche Erschließung geben u. a. Rudolf Haas und
   Alfred Weber (vgl. Literaturhinweise).
7 Vgl. Clüver (Anm. 4) S. 182.

als auch weil es als zu banal[8] betrachtet wurde. Den Grund für
diese divergierenden Urteile allein im Aufeinandertreffen ver-
schiedener weltanschaulicher Positionen zu suchen, wäre zu
einseitig, obwohl der christlich geprägte Humanismus des sich
der abendländischen Kultur verpflichtet fühlenden Wilder
sozialistisch orientierten Kritikern unannehmbar schien.
Wesentlicher ist es, die Strukturen und Inhalte seines Werkes
selbst auf ihre Aussagekraft hin zu befragen.

Die Form des Dramas *Our Town* allein ist schon bemerkens-
wert. Wilders konsequente Ablehnung der traditionellen
Guckkastenbühne unterscheidet es und unterschied es 1938 in
noch stärkerem Maße von vielem, was der Theaterzuschauer
zu sehen gewohnt ist und war. Wenngleich die formalen Mittel, die Wilder verwendet, nicht grundsätzlich innovatorisch
sind, so läßt sich doch der Feststellung zustimmen, daß hier
»geradezu ein Kompendium aller für die moderne Dramatik
typischen formalen Elemente«[9] zu finden ist. Eine leere
Bühne, die vor den Augen des Zuschauers mit ein paar Stüh-
len, Brettern und Spalieren ausgestattet wird, die Häuser,
Gärten, Straße, Kirche, Gräber bedeuten, ein Spielleiter, der
das Spiel als ein gespieltes im Bewußtsein hält, indem er die
Handlung kommentiert, mit der Vergangenheit und der
Zukunft frei schaltet und waltet und die Personen auf- und
abtreten läßt, die Einbeziehung des Publikums durch direkte
Anrede, das Auftreten von Toten – all dies sind Mittel, die die
Illusion durchbrechen, Distanz zum Dargestellten schaffen
und so dessen Reflexion begünstigen. Es liegt nahe, hier an
Brecht zu denken, an seine Theorie des nichtaristotelischen
Theaters und dessen aufklärerische Intention. Und in der Tat
lassen sich formale Anknüpfungspunkte bis ins Detail aufzei-
gen.[10] Dennoch wäre es verfehlt zu sagen, das Theater Wilders
sei dem Brechts wesensverwandt. Bei aller äußerlichen Ver-

---

8 Vgl. Schik (Anm. 5) S. 440 f.
9 Schimpf (Anm. 2) S. 30.
10 Vgl. Douglas C. Wixson jr., »The Dramatic Techniques of Thornton
    Wilder and Bertolt Brecht: A Study in Comparison«, in: *Modern Drama*
    15 (1972) S. 112–124.

gleichbarkeit ergibt sich doch ein Unbehagen bei der Feststellung von Gemeinsamkeiten, wie bei einer Gleichung, die nicht aufgeht. Nur wenn man das epische Theater als ein rein technisch bestimmtes versteht, ist der Vergleich ergiebig. Brecht selbst bezeugt dies, wenn er sagt, das epische Theater sei beinahe zu einem formalen Konzept geworden, das sich gleichermaßen auf Claudel und sogar auf Wilder anwenden ließe.[11] In dem »sogar« liegt jedoch die Kluft, die beide trennt. Das Unbehagen über die Verschiedenheit trotz offensichtlicher Ähnlichkeit, das Vergleiche in dem Resümee enden läßt, daß der Marxist Brecht sich von Wilder eben doch unterscheide,[12] oder in der fragwürdigen Formulierung, die Mittel des epischen Theaters seien wertneutral,[13] läßt sich auflösen, wenn man die kategoriale Verschiedenheit der beiden Werkkonzeptionen einbezieht. Während Brecht das epische Theater primär von seiner Wirkung her begründet, ist es für Wilder primär Darstellungsmöglichkeit, läßt ihn das auf die Bühne bringen und damit anschaulich machen, was seinem Wesen nach undramatisch ist. Denn das Grundthema des Wilderschen Werkes ist die Frage nach dem, was das menschliche Leben ausmacht. Wilders frühe Stücke, die sogenannten »Dreiminutenspiele«, die er bereits als Schüler zu schreiben begann, nähern sich dieser Frage, und zwar unter spezifisch christlicher Perspektive. Ein Prozeß zunehmender Abstrahierung ließ die Grundkategorien menschlicher Erfahrung, Raum und Zeit, immer stärker in den Vordergrund treten und brachte zugleich einen kühneren Umgang mit den dramaturgischen Mitteln, um

11 Vgl. Bertolt Brecht, *Notizen über die Dialektik auf dem Theater*, Bertolt-Brecht-Archiv, Mappe 23, Bl. 20, zitiert bei John Willett (Hrsg.), *Brecht on Theatre*, New York 1964, S. 281.
12 Vgl. auch Walter Hincks Urteil über Wilder: »Also im ganzen ein traditioneller, metaphysisch und auch christlich gebundener Humanismus, der dem revolutionären, auf durchgreifende gesellschaftliche Veränderungen gerichteten Humanismus Brechts sehr fern steht. Dort eine relativ quietistische, hier eine provokatorische Intention gegenüber Publikum und Gesellschaft. Und doch sind beide in der Anwendung gleicher dramaturgischer Mittel verbunden.« W. H., *Die Dramaturgie des späten Brecht*, Göttingen 1959, S. 148.
13 Vgl. Schik (Anm. 5) S. 440.

eben diesen Grundkategorien auf eine ihnen entsprechende Weise Ausdruck zu verleihen. Wichtige Beispiele für diese Entwicklung sind die bereits auf *Our Town* hinweisenden Einakter *The Long Christmas Dinner* (1931) und *Pullman Car Hiawatha* (1931).

In *The Long Christmas Dinner*, einem Stück, in dem vier aufeinanderfolgende Generationen einer Familie an einem Tisch beim Weihnachtsmahl sitzen, wird die Zeit selbst zum Thema; ihr Verstreichen wird offenbar im Auf- und Abtreten der Figuren durch die Türen der Geburt und des Todes, in ihrem Altern, dargestellt durch das Aufsetzen von grauen Perücken und durch die Hinweise auf die ablaufenden Jahre, die zwischen den Weihnachtsfesten liegen. Gleichzeitig jedoch erweist sich das an die Zeit gebundene menschliche Leben als konstant, die Weihnachtsfeste der aufeinanderfolgenden Generationen werden, wie schon der Titel besagt, als *ein* Weihnachtsmahl dargestellt, die Wiederholung des immer gleichen, der eine Tisch, die kaum variierte Unterhaltung, lassen alles Individuelle zurücktreten und aufgehen in einem Bild des Lebens schlechthin. Dieses Bild ist beruhigend und bedrückend zugleich; beruhigend, weil das Einzelschicksal eingebunden ist in ein sich selbst erhaltendes Kontinuum, symbolisiert durch den Verband der Familie; bedrückend aber, weil in der Perspektive der endlosen Zeit das Einzelschicksal klein wird, unbedeutend und sinnlos. Je mehr aber das Stück aufgrund seiner sich fortsetzenden Wiederholungen dieser zweiten Sichtweise zuneigt, desto deutlicher werden Verfallstendenzen in der Familie sichtbar. So wird die Zeit in diesem Stück zum Gegenspieler des Menschen, wird zum Akteur im dramatischen Konflikt, vor dessen Macht der Mensch zu erliegen scheint, ja der er zweifellos erläge, wenn ihm nicht die geringe Hoffnung bliebe, die die Rückwendung am Schluß aufscheinen läßt, welche durch Anknüpfung an den festgefügten Verband der Familie auf die sinngebende Kraft zwischenmenschlicher Beziehungen verweist. Mit den Worten »dear little Roderick and little Lucia«, die eine liebevolle

Verbundenheit der Alten mit den Jungen ausdrücken, endet das Stück.[14]

Deutlicher noch als *The Long Christmas Dinner* weist *Pullman Car Hiawatha* inhaltlich und formal auf *Our Town* hin, wenngleich es dem in seiner Verknappung und Konzentration eindrucksvollen ersteren Drama möglicherweise an Aussagekraft nachsteht. Hatte Wilder in jenem die Zeit auf der Bühne anschaulich werden lassen, so umspannt er hier Zeit und Raum und läßt das menschliche Leben als Teil des Universums erkennen. Die Reise durch das nächtliche Amerika wird zur Lebensfahrt, in der die Stunden selbst als Philosophen auftreten. Der Ort, ein Schlafwagen – durch Stühle und Kreidestriche auf dem Bühnenboden angedeutet – erfährt schon durch seinen Namen – ›Hiawatha‹ ist im Mythos der Indianer der Urheber von Kultur und Zivilisation – eine symbolische Überhöhung, er wird zur Stätte der zivilisierten Menschheit; die Himmelfahrt Hiawathas, die auch in dem geläufigen deutschen Titel *Schlafwagen Pegasus* anklingt, unterstreicht die Transzendierung des Raumes, die sich im Tod der Reisenden Harriet vollzieht. Den Kosmos auf die Bühne bringen zu wollen, wäre jedoch ein groteskes Unterfangen, wenn nicht deutlich würde, daß das, was dargestellt wird, Modell ist, daß das Theater in ganz konsequenter Nutzung seines ureigenen Gestus des Zeigens zum Material wird, aus dem das Modell gefertigt ist. Eine besondere Funktion fällt dabei der Figur des Spielleiters zu, der diesen Gestus aufrecht und im Bewußtsein der Zuschauer lebendig erhält. Er entwirft mit Kreidestrichen den Schlafwagen, er läßt die Figuren auf- und abtreten, er läßt sogar ihr Denken für das Publikum hörbar werden (»Now I want you to hear the thinking«, S. 52)[15]. Indem das Bühnengeschehen sich als Modell erkennen läßt, verweist es auf das, was an ihm deutlich werden soll; es ist, wie Marianne Kesting es

14 Vgl. die Interpretation von Wilhelm Rossi, in: W. Hüllen / W. Rossi / W. Christopeit (Hrsg.), *Zeitgenössische amerikanische Dichter*, Frankfurt a. M. 1960, S. 165–170.

15 Zitiert nach der Ausgabe: Thornton Wilder, *The Long Christmas Dinner and Other Plays in One Act*, New York: Harper and Row, 1963.

formuliert »von einem Theater der vorwiegend abbildenden Darstellung zu einem Theater der vorwiegend deutenden Darstellung vorgedrungen«.[16]

Daraus ergibt sich die Frage, wie sich die Deutung des Geschehens vollzieht, wie das Verhältnis von Darstellung und Deutung beschaffen ist. Dies geschieht zunächst durch explizite Verknüpfung zweier Realitätsebenen innerhalb des Spiels. Einerseits werden die Figuren als Schlafwagenreisende gezeigt, mit ihren banalen Problemen wie einer undichten Wärmflasche und ihren alltäglichen, um Berufsleben, Freundin oder Lebensversicherung kreisenden Gedankeninhalten, die man vernimmt, wenn sie vom Spielleiter abgerufen werden. Als eben diese Gedankeninhalte ein zweites Mal abgerufen werden, nun nicht in Einzelheiten hörbar, sondern als »thinking murmur«, ergibt sich andererseits, unterstützt durch die die Orte repräsentierenden Figuren »the earth's sound«, die Stimme der Erde, die in der vom Spielleiter dirigierten Sphärensymphonie erklingt. Das zweimalige »this is the earth's sound« (S. 64) des Spielleiters macht aus dem Trivialen der einzelnen Gedanken das Umfassende, Kosmische, ohne daß die innere Verbundenheit, ja Identität beider Ebenen aufgehoben würde. Aus dieser Verbundenheit heraus gewinnen die Hauptfiguren des Stückes, die geistesgestörte Frau und vor allem Harriet, ihre Bedeutung. Als die kosmische Symphonie erklingt, die jeden als Teil eines harmonischen Ganzen erscheinen läßt, beginnt die Geistesgestörte leidenschaftlich zu weinen und wendet sich an den Spielleiter mit den Worten: »Use me. Give me something to do.« (S. 64) Sie allein erfährt sich im Zusammenspiel aller als vereinzelt, als bedeutungslos. Ihre irdische Existenz erscheint ihr als Zustand des Wartens (»what possible use can there be in my simply waiting?«, S. 65), das Auftreten von Erzengeln, die die tote Harriet holen, erfüllt sie vorübergehend mit der Hoffnung, es gelte ihr. Was sie von den übrigen trennt, ist ihr geistiger Zustand, der den anderen als gestört, zurückgeblieben erscheint, von ihr

16 Marianne Kesting, *Das epische Theater*, Stuttgart [7]1978, S. 111.

selbst aber als ein tiefes Verstehen erfahren wird. Ihre eigene Existenz wird ihr bewußt, ebenso wie das Fehlen dieses Bewußtseins bei den übrigen (»At last I understand myself perfectly, but no one else understands a thing I say«, S. 65; »everyone is so childish, so absurd. They have no logic. These people are all so mad. These people are like children; they have never suffered«, S. 66). Indem sie hier all die Urteile, die sie selbst treffen, über die anderen fällt, erscheint das menschliche Vermögen der Einsicht und des Verstehens als bedingt, als nur in einem bestimmten Kontext richtig. Ändert sich die Perspektive, verändert sich der Anspruch auf Wahrheit. Am radikalsten ändert sich die Perspektive für Harriet durch ihren Tod. Als soeben Gestorbene, noch ganz Teil der irdischen Welt, bekräftigt sie dem Erzengel »I belong here« (S. 66), um nur kurz darauf in Tränen auszubrechen, als sie ihr Leben in Rückschau zu betrachten beginnt: »I haven't done anything with my life. [...] I never realized anything« (S. 66). Diese zentrale Stelle des Übergangs von der Perspektive der Lebenden zur Perspektive der Toten ist in diesem Spiel entschieden religiös geprägt. Harriet erfährt ihr vergangenes Leben als Schuld, verlangt nach Läuterung durch Strafe und ist nur allmählich bereit, ihren Tod als einen Vorgang der Erlösung anzunehmen. Letztendlich steht jedoch der Aspekt des Erkennens wieder im Vordergrund. Nach ihrem Abschied von der Welt ist sie, nun eine Wissende, bereit, diese endgültig zu verlassen. Sie wendet sich ab und geht mit den Worten »I see now. I see now. I understand everything now« (S. 68), worauf sich ihre Stimme nun über die erneut einsetzende Sphärenmusik erhebt. Auf die Ebene der Reisenden zurückversetzt, wird jedoch die Frage nach ihrem Befinden, nach dem Befinden derjenigen, die gesagt hatte »I want to be all new« (S. 67), mit dem lapidaren Satz beantwortet: »She ain't one jot better« (S. 69), wodurch das Verhältnis der Ebenen ironisch in der Schwebe gehalten wird, da die kranke Harriet nun tot ist, ihr Krankheitsverlauf also das schlimmste Ende gefunden hat, die tote Harriet aber dem Wunderbaren entgegensieht (»What wonderful things must be beginning now«, S. 67).

Mit seinen frühen Einaktern – und deshalb wurde hier relativ
ausführlich auf zwei der wichtigsten verwiesen – hat Wilder
sich eine Position geschaffen, von der aus er sein ›full length
play‹, das ihn als Dramatiker bekannt machte, nämlich *Our
Town*, gestalten konnte. Mittels der konsequenten Nutzung
des Bühnengeschehens als eines Modells sowie der sich aus
dem Gestus des Zeigens ergebenden epischen Form konnte er
nun darangehen, dem Zuschauer dessen eigene Welt zu prä-
sentieren. Grover's Corner ist nicht Abbild einer amerikanischen Kleinstadt des frühen zwanzigsten Jahrhunderts, sondern nutzt einige typische Elemente einer solchen, um Modell
sein zu können für Lebenswirklichkeit, die weit allgemeiner
ist, als die angegebenen Jahreszahlen vermuten lassen könnten. Nicht ganz zufällig sicher sind als Daten für die Handlung
des ersten und zweiten Aktes jeweils der 7. eines Monats
gewählt, Anklang an den siebten Schöpfungstag, die fertige,
von Menschen bevölkerte Welt, die sich der Betrachtung
darbietet. In *The Long Christmas Dinner* war der einzelne dem
sich erhaltenden Familienverband gegenübergestellt worden,
hier ist die Sehweise komplizierter geworden. Die Stadt bildet
die Konstante gegenüber dem einzelnen Bewohner, die
Schicksale ähneln sich, sie führen zu einem gemeinsamen
›man‹ zusammen; gleichzeitig steht jedoch die einzelne sich
wandelnde Stadt dem Kontinuum der Geschichte gegenüber,
Babylon wird erwähnt sowie die Griechen und Römer. Was
man von diesen weiß, sind ein paar akzidentielle Fakten, »the
names of the kings and some copies of wheat contracts«
(S. 32). Was man aber gleichermaßen weiß, ist, daß die Familien sich abends zum Essen zusammensetzten – Familienleben,
eine Grundstruktur der menschlichen Zivilisation, die unver-
ändert ist. Aus überlieferten Versen und Komödien kann man
sich einiges zusammenreimen, so heißt es, und so ist es doppelt
ironisch, wenn in dem Grundstein der neuen Bank eine Ausgabe von *Our Town* der Nachwelt erhalten bleiben soll: die
einfachen Tatsachen aus dem Alltagsleben spiegeln ja gerade
auch das Allgemeine, in den Jahrtausenden Unveränderte.

Zugleich aber wird der Zeigecharakter des Stückes selbst in dieser kleinen Pointe reflektiert.

Das Wechselspiel der Dimensionen, der Enge des Partikularen und der Weite des Universellen, durchzieht den gesamten ersten Akt. Dem rassischen Grobgefüge sowie den Durchschnittswerten der Geburten- und Sterblichkeitsrate steht die um zwei neugeborene Kinder zu erweiternde genaue Einwohnerzahl gegenüber, der minutiösen geographischen Festlegung des Ortes sowie der exakten Zeitangabe die ins Unabsehbare weisenden geologischen Formationen. So ergibt sich eine Ortung des Menschen und der Menschen, die am Ende des ersten Aktes in der Adresse des Briefes an Jane Crofut ihren Höhepunkt und Abschluß findet: Jane Crofut, das unbedeutende, im Stück gar nicht auftretende kleine Mädchen geht auf in einem kosmischen Raum, der sich im Geist Gottes ins Unendliche weitet. Gleichzeitig stellt die Benennung der einzelnen, von diesem unendlichen Raum aus betrachtet, deren ungeheure Bedeutung als Einzigartige dar. Das Teleskop mit seinen beiden Blickrichtungen, der verkleinernden und der vergrößernden, ist eines der Lieblingsbilder Wilders in diesem Zusammenhang und wird auch in dieser Szene ins Spiel gebracht. Die religiöse Deutung des kosmischen Raumes ist in diesem Stück ungleich verhaltener als in *Pullman Car Hiawatha*. Rebecca Gibbs zitiert die Adresse als den Einfall eines Pfarrers, womit sie ganz aus dem Kontext der Handlung heraus motiviert ist.

Die universelle Sicht des Stückes setzt sich fort in den ihm zugrunde liegenden Rhythmen der Natur, wie sie sich im Ablauf des Tages, der Jahreszeiten und auch im Ablauf des menschlichen Lebens zeigen. Der erste Akt spielt im Frühjahr, und die Handlung setzt ein, als Dr. Gibbs frühmorgens von der Geburt von Zwillingen zurückkehrt. Der zweite Akt ist dem Sommer gewidmet, der Zeit der Reife, dem Heranwachsen und der Heirat der Gibbs- und Webbkinder George und Emily. Der letzte Akt schließlich ist bestimmt durch den Tod und die ihm entsprechende Jahreszeit. Nicht Emilys Begräbnis jedoch findet im Winter statt, sondern der Tag, den sie auswählt, um noch einmal in ihr Leben zurückzukehren. Wie in der Grobstruktur des Stückes, so bleibt auch innerhalb der einzelnen Akte dieser Rhythmus bewußt: Geburt und Tod verbinden sich deutlich, da Emily im Kindbett stirbt; im ersten Akt wird unter Durchbrechung der Bühnengegenwart schon auf den Jahre später erfolgenden Tod der Hauptfiguren verwiesen, während der zweite Akt allgemeiner auf den Lebenskreislauf Bezug nimmt: »Summers and winters have cracked the mountains a little bit more and the rains have brought down some of the dirt. Some babies that weren't even born before have begun talking regular sentences already; and a number of people who thought they were right young and spry have noticed that they can't bound up a flight of stairs like they used to, without their heart fluttering a little« (S. 44). In diesen Kontext des allgemeinen Werdens und Vergehens der Menschen wird das Alltagsleben zweier Familien gestellt, das sich schon insofern in das Allgemeine einfügt, als die Familien deutliche Parallelen aufweisen. Nichts Außergewöhnliches geschieht an diesem 7. Mai, es ist ein Tag wie jeder andere – »daily life«, wie auch der erste Akt betitelt ist. Während dieser Akt also das Alltägliche zeigt: Frühstück, Schulgang, kleine typische Familienkonflikte, zeigt der zweite Akt ein singuläres Ereignis, die Hochzeit von Emily und George. Dennoch setzt das Spiel auch hier kaum individuelle Akzente: Das für den einzelnen Besondere erweist sich als das Übliche, Althergebrachte – »people are meant to go through life two by two« (S. 51). Erst der dritte Akt bringt – mit der Rückkehr der toten Emily ins Leben an einem Tag, der dem des ersten Aktes ähnelt – die Veränderung der Perspektive aus der heraus das Besondere des Lebens erkannt wird: »So all that was going on and we never noticed« (S. 93). Diese Erkenntnis gleicht der Harriets in *Pullman Car Hiawatha*, mit dem bedeutungsvollen Unterschied jedoch, daß Harriets Leben nicht Gegenstand des Dramas war. Emilys Leben ist aber in all seiner Trivialität soeben abgelaufen, worin soll das Unerkannte und jetzt als das Wesentliche Erscheinende liegen, das diese Umdeutung ermöglicht?

Hier ist wiederum der Modellcharakter des Stückes von ent-
scheidender Bedeutung, die Tatsache, daß dies kein abbilden-
des, sondern deutendes Theater ist. Der Spielleiter durch-
bricht ständig die Illusion, daß das Geschehen auf der Bühne
dargestellte Wirklichkeit sei, er bewegt sich frei inner- und
außerhalb der Spielhandlung, er konstituiert die Spielwirklich-
keit überhaupt erst. »This play is called "Our Town"« (S. 5),
beginnt er das Stück, stellt es als ein Spiel vor. Kurz darauf
heißt es: »The First Act shows a day in our town«, auch hier ist
der Spielcharakter noch präsent. Es wird etwas gezeigt. Dann
aber lautet der nächste Satz: »The day is May 7, 1901«. Der
eben noch als ein gezeigter eingeführte Tag ist jetzt durch den
Wechsel des Verbs von *show* zu *is* Bühnenwirklichkeit geworden. Ein akustisches Signal bestätigt dies: ein Hahn kräht. Auf
diese Weise sieht der Zuschauer das Stück beständig auf zwei
Ebenen. Er beobachtet das Alltagsleben zweier Familien,
gleichzeitig wird ihm dieses als etwas Dargestelltes, über sich
Hinausweisendes vermittelt. Diese doppelte Perspektive läßt
bereits eine Verbindung zur Sichtweise Emilys nach ihrem Tod
zu: »You not only live it; but you watch yourself living it«
(S. 86) beschreibt ihr der Spielleiter die Weise, wie sie ihr
eigenes Leben, in das sie zurückkehrt, erfahren wird. Es ist
jedoch noch ein Zwischenschritt zu tun, um die Verbindung
wirksam zu machen: Emily beobachtet ihr eigenes Leben, der
Zuschauer ein fremdes. Hier aber wird die Alltäglichkeit, die
Allgemeinheit des Dargestellten als Erkenntnismittel genutzt.
Explizit heißt es im zweiten Akt, bevor Emily und George
aufgefordert werden, die Szene im Drugstore vorzuspielen: »I
want you to try and remember what it was like to have been
very young. [. . .] Will you remember that, please?« (S. 57).
Der Zuschauer wird aufgefordert, seine eigene Erfahrung mit
der gespielten Szene zu verbinden, weil diese nur so für ihn
Bedeutung erlangen kann. Die auf diese Weise eingeführte
Szene ist für das Stück von besonderer Wichtigkeit. Auf der
Handlungsebene erfährt man hier, wie die nachbarliche Kame-
radschaft von George und Emily in eine Liebesgeschichte
einmündet, gewichtiger ist dieser Vorgang jedoch im Hinblick

auf seine Funktion für den thematischen Zusammenhang, der um die Frage nach der Möglichkeit, das Eigentliche des menschlichen Lebens zu erkennen, kreist. Emily wirft George vor, er sei eingebildet und unliebenswürdig geworden. Sie will seine Gefühle nicht verletzen, aber sie hält es für ihre Pflicht, ihm die Wahrheit zu sagen (»I'm sorry if that hurts your feelings, but I've got to – tell the truth and shame the devil«, S. 59). Die plötzliche Erkenntnis ihres Gefühles für George jedoch läßt sie unsicher in ihrer Meinung werden, ihre ursprüngliche Erwartung, ein Mann habe vollkommen zu sein, relativiert sich, sie weiß plötzlich, daß das, was sie vorher für Wahrheit hielt, nicht die Wahrheit ist. Ihre Sehweise hat sich verändert. Das vorher Wichtige ist unbedeutend geworden: »Now I can see it's not the truth at all. And I suddenly feel that it isn't important, anyway« (S. 60). Dieser Prozeß wird noch gespiegelt in dem, was George erfährt. Er plant, die landwirtschaftliche Hochschule zu besuchen, bittet Emily, ihm Briefe zu schreiben, und beschließt plötzlich, in Grover's Corner zu bleiben. Auch hier ist das vorher Wichtige unbedeutend geworden, anderes hat statt dessen an Wichtigkeit gewonnen – das Wort *important* zieht sich wie ein roter Faden durch die Szene. »Life's awfully funny!«, kommentiert Emily ihre neue Sehweise, während George deutlicher das zum Ausdruck bringen will, was nun wichtig ist: »I think that once you've found a person that you're fond of [. . .]. Well, I think that's just as important as college is, and even more so. That's what I think. – EMILY. I think it's awfully important, too« (S. 64). Verschiedene Motivstränge des Stückes werden in diesem »important talk« aufgenommen. Das Bedeutsame im Kontrast zum Gleichgültigen klang bereits in Dr. Gibbs' Abneigung gegen das Reisen an (»No, he said, it might make him discontented with Grover's Corner to go traipsin' about Europe«, S. 20). Er zieht statt dessen die Schlachtfelder des Sezessionskrieges vor, seine unmittelbare Umgebung, seine amerikanische Welt sind ihm wichtig. Hier läßt sich ein Bogen schlagen zu dem Verhältnis des Kleinen, Unbedeutenden, Einzelnen zur kosmischen Gesamtheit. So sinnlos das einzelne vor dem

Hintergrund des Ganzen scheinen mag, so sinnvoll ist es doch, wenn es aufgrund einer sinngebenden Beziehung aus seiner Anonymität entlassen wird; die Spanne von Jane Crofut zum Geist Gottes liefert hier die Perspektive.

Der Schluß von *The Long Christmas Dinner* hatte bereits auf die Bedeutung der liebevollen Beziehung des Familienverbandes angesichts des Kontinuums der Zeit hingewiesen, in *Our Town* wird, solchermaßen betrachtet, das alltägliche Familienfrühstück zum Paradigma mütterlicher Liebe und Wärme. Wenn Thornton Wilder in seinem späteren Drama *The Alcestiad or A Life in the Sun* Alcestis sagen läßt: »Love is not the meaning. It is one of the signs that there is a meaning«, so steht dies in ebendemselben Kontext des Zusammenhanges von Liebe und Erkenntnis dessen, was wesentlich ist. Mutter Gibbs, die selbst ein zugelaufenes Küken mit menschlicher Güte behandelt, die wie eine Glucke (»You're losin' one of your chicks«, S. 49) ihre Kinder umsorgt – die Empfehlung an George, seine eigenen Küken nach dem ›Philo‹-System aufzuziehen, ist eine versteckte und humorvolle Fortführung dieses Bildes –, vermag auch der toten Emily Wege zum Verständnis des Seins zu eröffnen. Verstärkt wird dieser Aspekt der zwischenmenschlichen Beziehungen noch durch das Lied »Blessed Be the Tie That Binds«[17], das leitmotivisch das ganze Stück durchzieht.

Die Verbindung der Sehweise von Emily und George, die auf deren noch radikalere Veränderung nach Emilys Tod hinweist, wird durch die Bedeutung des gesamten Aktes »Love and Marriage« unterstützt. Was in der Drugstoreszene als Vorausschau auf Emilys spätere Erfahrung im Rahmen des Beziehungsgeflechtes von Liebe, Lebenssinn und Erkenntnis begon-

---

17 Ein in Amerika sehr bekanntes Kirchenlied von John Fawcett (1739–1817). Der Text lautet: »Blessed be the tie that binds / Our hearts in Christian love; / The fellowship of kindred minds / Is like to that above. // Before our Father's throne / We pour our ardent prayers; / Our fears, our hopes, our aims are one, / Our comforts and our cares. // We share each other's woes, / Each other's burdens bear. / And often for each other flows / The sympathizing tear. // When we are called to part / It gives us inward pain, / But we shall still be joined in heart, / And hope to meet again.«

nen wurde, findet einen weiteren Kulminationspunkt in der Hochzeit selbst, die durch verschiedene, scheinbar belanglose Motive mit dem Tod im dritten Akt verknüpft ist. »[...] if a person starts out to be a teacher, she ought to stay one« (S. 11), erklärt der junge Joe Crowell anläßlich der bevorstehenden Eheschließung seiner Lehrerin, wodurch das Motiv der Hochzeit und das damit verbundene Thema der Wandlung des Menschen erstmals anklingt. Und »Only five more hours to live« (S. 52) sagt George vor seiner Trauung in einer, von ihm durchaus scherzhaft gesehenen Verbindung von Heirat und Tod. In der Szene vor der Trauung, die ihrerseits ein Abbild der zuvor gesprächsweise vorgestellten Situation der Hochzeit der Eltern Gibbs ist, wird diese Verbindung vertieft. Dr. Gibbs hatte in Erinnerung an seine Eheschließung gesagt: »And when I saw you comin' down that aisle I thought you were the prettiest girl I'd ever seen, but the only trouble was that I'd never seen you before. There I was in the Congregational Church marryin' a total stranger« (S. 50). Dieses Gefühl der Entfremdung erfahren auch George und Emily. In der Szene, in der unter Anlehnung an Freudsche Psychologie[18] die Gedanken der beiden offenbar werden, sehen sie nicht nur den anderen auf eine ganz veränderte Weise (»I *hate* him«, S. 70), sondern erfahren den Schritt, den sie zu tun beabsichtigen, als eine Entfremdung von ihrem eigenen alten Selbst (»Ma, I don't want to grow old«, S. 69; »All I want to do is to be a fella –«, S. 70; »But, Papa, – I don't want to get married. [...] Why can't I stay for a while just as I am?«, S. 70). So wird hier die Eheschließung zum Bild einer erneuerten Existenz, in der die Notwendigkeit der sinngebenden Kraft der Liebe erkannt wird (»I love you, Emily. I need you. EMILY. Well, if you love me, help me. All I want is someone to love me«, S. 71). Das zwischen den Polen der Bedeutungslosigkeit und Einzigartigkeit oszillierende Bild des einzelnen, dem der erste Akt in der ›Jane Crofut‹-Adresse Gestalt verliehen hatte, scheint erneut, jetzt aus der Handlung des Stückes, auf, lebensimmanent,

18 Vgl. Clüver (Anm. 4) S. 173.

doch mit deutlichem Anklang an ein über Immanenz hinausgehendes, das Singuläre mit dem Universellen verbindendes Lebensprinzip: »And I mean for *ever*. Do you hear? For ever and ever« (S. 71). »Love Divine, All Love Excelling« sowie »Blessed Be the Tie That Binds« bilden den motivischen Bezugsrahmen.

In dem bereits erwähnten, auf dem griechischen Alkestis-Mythos basierenden Stück *The Alcestiad* will Alcestis den König Admetus nicht heiraten, um sich ganz dem Dienst des Gottes Apollo zu weihen, erfährt aber dann, daß sich gerade im Menschlichen das Göttliche zeigt. Aufgrund dieser Erkenntnis ist sie befähigt, Admetus durch das Opfer ihres Lebens aus Liebe dem Tod zu entreißen. Was sich dort als singuläres Ereignis, als Bild idealer Liebe abspielt, wird in *Our Town* vom Spielleiter in die Sphäre des Alltäglichen zurückgerufen: M. . . . marries N. . . . millions of them. [. . .] Once in a thousand times it's interesting« (S. 73), so daß das Singuläre als Möglichkeit des Allgemeinen, nicht aber als dessen Wesensgesetz erscheint. Dieses schwebende Verhältnis von Wirklichkeit und Möglichkeit bestimmt aber zentral die Aussage des dritten Aktes. Im dritten Akt wird das, was dem Zuschauer bereits nahegebracht wurde, indem die agierenden Figuren vom Spielleiter schon zu Anfang als in der Gegenwart des Aufführungszeitpunktes bereits Tote vorgestellt wurden und indem er aufgefordert wurde, seine eigene Erinnerung in das Dargestellte hineinzutragen, unmittelbar auf die Bühne gebracht. Emily stirbt und erlebt eine Rückkehr in ihr Leben, erlebt noch einmal einen unbedeutenden Tag – das Motiv des »important« wird hier wieder aufgenommen –, erlebt ihn aber auf doppelte Weise: als Teilnehmende und als Beobachterin, die die Zukunft bereits kennt. Was ist nun das eigentlich Bedeutende des menschlichen Lebens? Die Toten befinden sich in einem Zustand, der durch eben das gekennzeichnet ist, was die Lebenden zu vermeiden suchen: Dr. Gibbs will nicht reisen, damit ihm seine eigene kleine Welt nicht unwichtig wird; George will nicht fort, weil er das Wichtige in der Liebe zu Emily gefunden hat, für die Toten aber ist nichts wichtig: »they

lose hold of the earth . . . and the ambitions they had . . . and
the pleasures they had . . . and the things they suffered . . . and
the people they loved« (S. 77). Sie werden gleichgültig, und die
so wichtigen Dinge verblassen (»all those terribly important
things kind of grow pale around here«, S. 78). Was für sie
wichtig ist, ist etwas anderes: »Something important, and
great. Aren't they waitin' for the eternal part in them to come
out clear?« (S. 77). Sie gehören nun ganz zur Seite des Allgemeinen, Universellen. Sie verlieren alles Individuelle, Besondere: »And what's left when memory's gone, and your identity, Mrs. Smith?« (S. 78). Unter diesem Aspekt gewinnt das
Leben eine neue Perspektive: es wird als ein durch seine
Begrenzung bestimmtes gesehen. Die Begrenzung bestimmt
das Singuläre des Menschen, enthüllt aber auch seine
Beschränktheit. Dieser Aspekt ist der erste, der thematisiert
wird, Emilys erste Erkenntnis beim Eintritt in die Welt der
Toten: »They're sort of shut up in little boxes, aren't they?»
(S. 84). Die äußere Begrenztheit des Lebens, die Bezogenheit
auf das eigene Selbst korrespondieren mit einer Begrenztheit
der Sehweise, die Emily bei der Rückkehr in die Welt erfährt.
»I can't look at everything hard enough« (S. 90) und »Oh,
Mama, just look at me one minute as though you really saw
me« (S. 91) ist Ausdruck dieses Unvermögens und mündet in
die abschließende Frage: »Do any human beings ever realize
life while they live it?« (S. 93). *Realize* ist hier noch umfassen-
der als *look* und *see*, es verbindet sehen, erkennen, begreifen
und verwirklichen.[19]

Leben erscheint hier als grundsätzlich ambivalent: einerseits
als Blindheit, Unwissenheit, Egoismus und sinnlose Ver-
schwendung der aufgrund ihrer Begrenztheit kostbaren Zeit.
So sieht es vor allem Simon Stimson, dessen Leben von Nöten
gezeichnet war und der im Selbstmord den einzigen Ausweg
sah. Er erinnert an die geistesgestörte Frau in *Pullman Car
Hiawatha*, die – Außenseiter und Leidende wie er – zu besonderer Erkenntnis befähigt war. Dramaturgisch geschickter

19 Vgl. Helmut Viebrock, »Thornton Wilders Hauptmotiv«, in: *Die Neueren
Sprachen* 10 (1961) S. 356.

wird Stimson hier allein die negative Sicht zugewiesen, so daß
die Ambivalenz des Lebens plastischer wird. Die Blindheit der
Lebenden ist andererseits offensichtlich notwendig, um das
Leben überhaupt ertragen zu können, das von einer solchen
Tiefe und Fülle ist, daß es gar nicht ganz erfaßt werden kann.
Schon das Alltägliche ist in den Augen der nun Sehenden so
überwältigend, daß sie ihm willig den Rücken kehrt. Das
Motiv des Abschieds, das in *Pullman Car Hiawatha* anklang,
hat sich hier entscheidend geändert. Nicht das Empfinden
persönlicher Schuld ist es, das den Abschied vom Leben
kennzeichnet, sondern das Erkennen, nicht richtig gelebt zu
haben, was aber paradoxerweise zugleich als das Wesensmerkmal des Lebens selbst gesehen wird. Nur in Momenten kann
ein Mehr aufscheinen, wie in dem Gefühl, gemeinsam glück-
lich zu sein (»But, just for a moment now we're all together.
Mama, just for a moment we're happy«, S. 92), so fragwürdig
das wirkliche Empfinden dieses Glückes auch immer ist.
»Wherever you come near the human race, there's layers and
layers of nonsense« (S. 76), sagt der Spielleiter, das menschliche Leben ist geradezu gekennzeichnet durch das Unsinnige,
Unbedeutende. Und dennoch – »look at that star« (S. 94), rät
Mrs. Gibbs der verstörten Emily, die durch Simon Stimson in
ihrem negativen Bild des menschlichen Lebens bestärkt wird.
Die Sterne, die Millionen Lichtjahre von der Erde entfernt
sind, die unablässig ihre Bahnen ziehen, sind Sinnbild eines
geordneten Ganzen, in denen der eine Stern, der belebte, eine
besondere Stelle einnimmt, weil er sich müht, etwas aus sich zu
machen (»Only this one is straining away, straining away all
the time to make something of itself«, S. 95).
In *Pullman Car Hiawatha* hatte sich das Bühnengeschehen
deutlich als Modell des Universums gezeigt, das als Sphärensymphonie dem Zuschauer vorgeführt werden konnte. In *Our
Town* stützt sich die Aussage, ohne daß dadurch etwas von
dem Modellcharakter des Stückes aufgegeben würde, in weit
stärkerem Maße auf die Handlung selbst. Ein Wesensmerkmal
des Dramas vor allem ist es, das diesem sublimeren Modell
zugute kommt. Es ist die Tatsache, daß Drama beständig

Gegenwart ist. Aus dem Spannungsverhältnis zwischen der als gegenwärtig erscheinenden Handlung und dem durch den Spielleiter vermittelten Kontext der Vergangenheit und Zukunft, des Momentes und der ungeheueren Spannweite der Zeit ergibt sich das Verhältnis von Zeigen und Bedeuten, das sich im gesprochenen Wort als einem handlungsimmanent motivierten wie auch als einem im Sinne des Modells verweisenden wiederholt. Würde die Handlung nicht als modellhaft deutlich, fiele sie in sich zusammen. Wenn eingangs gesagt wurde, daß Wilder seinem Wesen nach Undramatisches darstellt, so findet sich das hier bestätigt. Die Handlung hat aus sich heraus keine dramatische Substanz, keinen Konflikt, der auf vielschichtigere Bedeutungszusammenhänge verweisen könnte. Unter der Voraussetzung des Modells jedoch bezieht er seine dramatische Spannung aus der epischen Form. Wilder entband, wie Szondi es formuliert, »die Handlung der dramatischen Aufgabe, aus ihrer inneren Gegensätzlichkeit die Form zu bilden, und übertrug sie einer neuen Gestalt, die außerhalb des thematischen Bereichs, am archimedischen Punkt des Epikers steht und in das Stück als Spielleiter eingeführt wird«.[20]

Wilder selbst umschreibt diesen Zusammenhang in einem Vorwort zu den *Three Plays*[21] und unterstellt ihn der Forderung an den Künstler nach Wahrheit. Ausgehend von der menschlichen Erfahrung, daß das, was dem einzelnen als Einzigartiges widerfährt, sich in der Menschheit unzählige Male wiederholt, stellt er die Frage, welche Wahrheit vorzuziehen sei, die der isolierten Begebenheit oder die, die das Zahllose einschließt: »As an artist (or listener or beholder) which ›truth‹ do you prefer – that of the isolated occasion, or that which includes and resumes the innumerable?«[22] Und er stellt fest, das Theater sei in besonderer Weise geeignet, beides zu vermitteln

20 Peter Szondi, *Theorie des modernen Dramas*, in: P. S., *Schriften I*, Frankfurt a. M. 1978 (suhrkamp taschenbuch wissenschaft 129), S. 127.
21 Thornton Wilder, *Three Plays: Our Town / The Skin of Our Teeth / The Matchmaker*, New York: Harper, 1957.
22 Ebd., S. X.

(»The theatre is admirably fitted to tell both truths«[23]). Dies sei das Entscheidende, nicht dagegen eine vordergründige Lebensechtheit, die er der Guckkastenbühne mit ihren realistischen Details vorwirft. Wirklichkeit, nicht Wahrscheinlichkeit ist sein Ziel (»not verisimilitude but reality«[24]). Wenn er jedoch feststellt, daß es die besondere Fähigkeit des Theaters sei, die dargestellte individuelle Handlung in das Reich der Idee, des Typus und des Universellen zu erheben (»the theatre's power to raise the exhibited individual action into the realm of idea and type and universal«[25]), und eben dieses dem traditionellen Theater abspricht, so läßt er die Möglichkeiten des dramatischen Konfliktes außer acht, der zu keiner Zeit als nur schöner Schein verstanden werden sollte und wollte, und wendet sich eher gegen überholte Inszenierungsformen und ungenügende Rezeptionsweisen als gegen die Sache selbst. Was Wilder vom traditionellen Theater unterscheidet, ist nicht ein Mehr oder Weniger an Wahrheit, sondern die Entscheidung, die Aussage des Stückes mittels eines Modells und nicht mittels einer dramatischen Handlung darzustellen.

Daß das Modell wirksam werden kann, liegt nicht allein an der Form seiner Vermittlung, sondern daran, daß das zu Vermittelnde elementare Grundfragen des menschlichen Lebens berührt, die Reduktion und Abstrahierung erfordern. So kann auch ein gemeinsames Bewußtsein der Zuschauer vorausgesetzt und auf gemeinsame Erfahrung verwiesen werden. Dies hat nichts zu tun mit Pseudodemokratisierung oder Verschleierung von Gegensätzen, was dem Stück gelegentlich vorgeworfen wird; denn das Ziel des Interesses liegt noch vor aller Gegensätzlichkeit, betrifft die ›conditio humana‹, und nicht die durch Divergenz gekennzeichnete Lebenswirklichkeit. Die Stelle im Stück, die von Kritikern vielfach als Stein des Anstoßes betrachtet wird, nämlich die Zuschauerfrage nach sozialer Ungerechtigkeit in Grover's Corner (S. 25), ist zu wörtlich, zu handlungsimmanent verstanden, wenn man aus ihr man-

23 Ebd., S. XI.
24 Ebd., S. XII.
25 Ebd., S. XI.

gelndes soziales Bewußtsein abliest. Vielmehr enthält diese Textstelle gerade einen Hinweis darauf, daß es hier nicht um Spiegelung sozialer Wirklichkeit geht. Die Replik des Spielleiters, daß Geldhaben oder -nichthaben ein Thema des Stadtklatsches sei, ist ebenso ironisch wie seine Bemerkung am Anfang, daß die Spaliere ein bißchen Szenerie für die ergäben, die nicht ganz ohne solche auskommen könnten (S. 8). Handlung und Bühnenausstattung werden gleichermaßen ihrer Eigenständigkeit enthoben, die Evidenz ihrer Funktionalität ist für die Bedeutung des Stückes unerläßlich.

Wenn Wilder sagt, Mythos, Parabel und Fabel seien der Urquell aller Fiktion, und dem Drama darin noch einen Vorzug vor dem Roman gibt,[26] so geht es ihm um jenen Verweischarakter, der aus dem Besonderen eine allgemeine Wahrheit oder eine Lehre aufscheinen läßt. Dies hat seine Berechtigung für *Our Town*, wenn man eben diese Tendenz zum Allgemeinen zum wesentlichen Vergleichspunkt macht. Der Vergleich mit den genannten Gattungen muß jedoch eine Einschränkung erfahren, wenn man deren Formgesetze einbezieht. Denn die Eigenständigkeit des Erzählten, die gerade typisch für Fabel und Parabel ist, ihre Abgeschlossenheit und innere Schlüssigkeit, die der Möglichkeit der Übertragung auf die Bedeutungsebene zugrunde liegen muß, wird in *Our Town* durch seinen Modellcharakter gerade durchbrochen. Der Bezug zum Mythos mag hier näherliegen, da dieser ja auch nicht an eine literarische Form gebunden ist. Das Archetypische im Stoff und der ins Rituelle verweisende, als erforderlich vorausgesetzte Konsensus des Publikums in Wilders Stück sowie seine Anklänge an das aus dem Kult erwachsene antike Drama sind verschiedentlich aufgezeigt und für die Interpretation fruchtbar gemacht worden.[27] Das Archetypische erhält bei Wilder eine gültige Form im modernen Drama. Die Anbindung von Grundfragen des menschlichen Lebens an das Drama als

---

26 Thornton Wilder, »Some Thoughts on Playwriting«, in: Toby Cole (Hrsg.), *Playwrights on Playwriting*, New York 1960, S. 108 f.

27 Vgl. Thomas E. Porter, »A Green Corner of the Universe: *Our Town*«, in: T. P., *Myth and Modern American Drama*, Detroit 1969, S. 200–224.

Modell führt in der Tat zu dem, was er vom Drama schlechthin fordert, nämlich glaubhaft zu sein.[28] Wie gesehen, wird das Modell nur da wirksam, wo es auch als solches offenbar wird. Diese Erfahrung enthält die Forderung nach absoluter Konsequenz in der Darstellung, wie sich vor allem auch dort zeigt, wo die Gefahr besteht, daß die Form des Dramas ihrem eigenen Anspruch nicht bis ins letzte Genüge tut. Wenn Emily am Ende ihres wiederdurchlebten Tages sagt: »Oh, earth, you're too wonderful for anybody to realize you« (S. 93), so gerät das Besondere der Handlung in bedrohliche Nähe dessen, was das Stück gar nicht sein will, nämlich der expliziten Botschaft an den Zuschauer. Dies widerspricht dem Modellcharakter, es stünde dann nicht Handlung für etwas anderes, sondern wollte selbst ihre eigene Deutung sein. In der Konsequenz einer solchen Auffassung fände man hier tatsächlich eine Verherrlichung des Trivialen, wie es dem Stück vorgeworfen worden ist, die Frage nach der Tiefe der menschlichen Existenz würde zur Platitüde, das Alltagsleben der Gibbs' und Webbs würde in seiner anheimelnden Alltäglichkeit zum Idealbild des Lebens schlechthin. Aus einer Stelle wie der zitierten wird die Gefahr eines solchen Mißverständnisses deutlich, weil sich aus dem Kontext heraus eine Lebensweisheit isolieren läßt; dies jedoch ist nicht typisch für die Struktur des Stückes, sondern widerspricht gerade seiner Form.

Ein Modell ist niemals identisch mit dem, was es zeigt, sondern sucht dessen Wesentliches in einem anderen, sinnfälligen Medium deutlich zu machen. Damit ist es zugleich Denkmodell, das auf Erkenntnis zielt, sich aber bewußt ist, daß es letztlich in der Natur des zu Erkennenden liegt, sich nicht festschreiben zu lassen. Die begeisterte Aufnahme, die *Our Town* im Nachkriegsdeutschland fand, läßt sich vordergründig als Ausdruck einer emotionalen Sehnsucht aufgrund der Erfahrungen von Faschismus und Krieg verstehen.[29] Sicherlich

28 Vgl. Wilder, *Three Plays* (Anm. 21) S. VII f., XI.

29 Vgl. Joseph C. Schöpp, »Thornton Wilders *Our Town*: theoretischer Anspruch und künstlerische Realisierung«, in: A. Weber / S. Neuweiler (Hrsg.), *Amerikanisches Drama und Theater im 20. Jahrhundert*, Göttingen 1975, S. 166.

mag der Wunsch nach einem friedlichen, behaglichen Alltagsleben die Rezeption mitbestimmt haben. Andererseits kann
das Interesse an dem Stück als Beleg dafür gelten, daß es
mittels seines Modellcharakters einer Bereitschaft zur Ausein-
andersetzung mit der Frage nach dem Eigentlichen des
menschlichen Lebens entgegenkam, daß die Reflexion tiefer
ging und nicht bei dankbarer Annahme ersehnten Trostes
verharrte. Heute scheint diese Wirkung des Stückes nachgelas-
sen zu haben, es ist von den Spielplänen weitgehend verdrängt,
das Innovatorische seiner Form ist schon fast historisch geworden und steht in der Kritik hinter dem Konservativen seines
Gehaltes zurück. Will man dem Stück auch heute noch (oder
wieder) ein adäquates Verständnis abgewinnen, so kann dies
nur geschehen, indem man das vermeidet, was man der Rezeption der fünfziger Jahre vielfach fälschlich zugeschrieben hat,
nämlich das Stück als ein nostalgisches Abbild der Wirklichkeit
zu betrachten. Wenn es dem zwanzigsten Jahrhundert zufiel,
»wieder im Paradigmatischen die Poesie zu entdecken«[30], so
setzt die Frage nach dem Wert dieser Poesie eine stets neue
Annahme des Paradigmatischen voraus.

Eva-Maria König

30 Volker Klotz, »Thornton Wilders *Unsere kleine Stadt*«, in: *Das neue
   Forum* 9 (1959/60) S. 64.

Inhalt

Our Town 4

Editorische Notiz 96
Literaturhinweise 97
Zeittafel 102
Nachwort 105

Fremdsprachentexte

IN RECLAMS UNIVERSAL-BIBLIOTHEK

Englische und amerikanische Dramen

Auswahl

Samuel Beckett: Waiting for Godot. 147 S. UB 9214

Brendan Behan: The Hostage. 141 S. UB 9222

Edward Bond: Summer. 104 S. UB 9197

John Gay: The Beggar's Opera. 143 S. UB 9228

Arthur Miller: The Crucible. 224 S. UB 9257 – Death of a Salesman. 171 S. UB 9172

Eugene O'Neill: Long Day's Journey into Night. 216 S. UB 9252

John Osborne: The Entertainer. 143 S. UB 9191

J. B. Priestley: An Inspector Calls. 117 S. UB 9218

Willy Russell: Educating Rita. 132 S. UB 9040

Peter Shaffer: Amadeus. 199 S. UB 9219

William Shakespeare: Hamlet. 261 S. UB 9292 – Macbeth. 167 S. UB 9220 – A Midsummer Night's Dream. 160 S. UB 9247 – Romeo and Juliet. 219 S. UB 9005

Bernard Shaw: Mrs Warren's Profession. 198 S. UB 9166 – Pygmalion. 197 S. UB 9266

Tom Stoppard: Rosencrantz and Guildenstern are Dead. 171 S. UB 9185

John Millington Synge: The Playboy of the Western World. 128 S. UB 9211

Oscar Wilde: The Importance of Being Earnest. 141 S. UB 9267 – Lady Windermere's Fan. 101 S. UB 9187

Thornton Wilder: Our Town. 127 S. UB 9168

Tennessee Williams: Cat on a Hot Tin Roof. 224 S. UB 9039 – The Glass Menagerie. 149 S. UB 9178 – A Streetcar Named Desire. 199 S. UB 9240

Philipp Reclam jun. Stuttgart